Playbook

for

Gridiron
GOSPEL

Faith That Moves Chains

LEONARD SWEET

The Salish
Sea Press
Orcas Island
Washington

Playbook for Gridiron Gospel: Faith That Moves Chains

ISBN: 978-1-63613-041-5

Published by The Salish Sea Press. Box 1492, Absecon, NJ 08201.
https://salishsea.press
https://www.facebook.com/thesalishseapress/

The Salish Sea Press is a program of SpiritVenture Ministries.
https://leonardsweet.com/

Copyright © 2025 by Leonard Sweet. All rights reserved.

Interior designed by Carmen Barber | keepingyouwriting@gmail.com
Cover designed by by Anthony Gorrity, Johnnyo Design | johnnyodesign.com

Unless otherwise indicated, Scripture quotations are the author's own paraphrase. If the notation LIS is used, this also indicates the author's own paraphrase. Other versions are noted in the back matter.

The Salish Sea Press

Dedicated to my fellow gospellers

Contents

Pregame Setup 7

Game I
First Down, First Love
Touchdowns in the Kingdom 11

Game II
The Divine Handoff
When God Calls the Play 27

Game III
From the Sidelines to the Stars
Rediscovering Faith in a Faithless Game 39

Game IV
Two Minute Warning
Divine Timing 53

Game V
Breaking Huddle
Steps of Faith 67

Game VI
Resilient Roots
The Enduring Triumph of Faith and Football 81

Game VII
Heaven's Scoreboard
Measuring What Matters 97

Game VIII
The Lombardi Legacy
Discipline as Devotion 111

Game IX
The Belichick Blueprint
Strategy and Spirit 127

GAME X
CROSSING THE GOAL LINE
WHERE HEAVEN MEETS EARTH 143

GAME XI
RED ZONE REDEMPTION
FROM FUMBLES TO FAITH...................................... 161

GAME XII
PLAYING INJURED
GRACE UNDER PRESSURE 171

GAME XIII
THE ULTIMATE CHAMPIONSHIP
BUILDING GOD'S TEAM 183

GAME XIV
WHEN TAILGATES BECOME TALEGATE TESTAMENTS
FELLOWSHIP IN THE PARKING LOT 195

GAME XV
MORE THAN GAMES
FROM ARENA TO ALTAR... 207

GAME XVI
BEYOND THE GOALPOSTS
FROM KICKOFF TO KINGDOM COME........................ 219

GAME XVII
LATERALS OF LOVE
PASSING FAITH THROUGH LIFE'S CHAOS 229

THE VICTORY CELEBRATION 241
FOURTH DOWN FAITH AND HAIL MARY HOPE 241

SCRIPTURE VERSIONS 247

ADDITIONAL STUDY QUESTIONS........................ 249

CONNECT WITH LEONARD.................................. 253

PREGAME SETUP

Welcome to the playbook to accompany *Gridiron Gospel: Faith that Moves Chains* by Leonard Sweet and Chris Erikson. Designed for small-group discussions throughout the NFL season, Leonard wrote this playbook to spark discussion and personal study. It has seventeen "Games" or chapters, each focusing on ways to make kingdom advances.

This playbook can be used in various ways, with most groups finding it best to have members commit to meeting each week for the season and choosing a group facilitator to help keep things on track. Though the playbook was designed with men in mind, the author joyfully acknowledges that many women share a love for the game and will be cherished voices in the group experience.

This playbook will be valuable to anyone, anywhere on their kingdom journey. At times, biblical references may be unfamiliar—a Bible concordance or other reference can help. Mark these

SWEET

areas for later study, or take a time out to explore the reference as a group.

Groups may meet at the same location each week or rotate through different places. Members may want to keep a prayer journal to record prayer requests and answers. This playbook is the springboard for creating a gathering that best meets the group's needs.

Each week, the playbook is divided into four main sections: Pregame, Halftime, Postgame, and Personal Training Session.

Pregame is a time to gather before kickoff. It includes:

- A warmup prayer
- A reflection on the previous week's Chain-Moving Challenge
- A Highlight Reel, which provides a summary of the *Gridiron Gospel: Faith that Moves Chains* chapter
- An overall theme or "Game Strategy" to set the focus for the day

The Halftime Huddle section includes discussion questions for the group to use, as desired, during the game's halftime. The group leader may preselect a few things to discuss, or members may help choose

PREGAME SETUP

items. If any topic warrants further discussion, it can be marked and revisited after the game.

The Postgame section provides:

- A discussion guide with points to ponder and questions to talk through as a group
- A Chain-Moving Challenge to help you apply these ideas and make kingdom advances through the next week
- A Postgame closing prayer

Finally, the Personal Training Session gives you further points to ponder, study, and apply during the coming week.

Additionally, there are some optional extra study questions at the back of the book.

So—are you ready for some football?

Game 1

First Down, First Love

Touchdowns in the Kingdom

Pregame

Warmup Prayer

Divine Coach of Our Being,
As we take the field of life each day,
Grant us dedication like athletes who study their playbook and the wisdom to recognize that Your Word is our ultimate game plan.

Help us find grace in our differences and joy in our shared faith,
Even when our earthly loyalties divide us.
Give us the strength to be more than spectators in your kingdom's great game,
Knowing that while the victory is secured through Christ,

SWEET

Each play still matters in your divine design.

Help us run with purpose toward the goal line,
Not as mere fans in the stands,
But as gospellers on your gridiron,
By faith, moving chains with every step.

May we play with the intensity of champions and
    the humility of servants,
Remembering that in your stadium,
Every down is a chance for eternal victory.

In the name of our Ultimate Victor,
Amen.

Chain-Moving Challenge Reflection

As you prepared for this first gathering, did you have any thoughts or goals for yourself or the group?

Highlight Reel

Game One introduces the intersection of faith and football in US culture, using both as lenses to understand deeper truths. The opening establishes football as more than just a sport. It's portrayed as a sacred ritual that shapes communities and calendars, much like religious observances.

The authors introduce this concept through the story of Richard and Jane Jameson, a faithful Christian couple whose marriage navigates the divided loyalties between Tennessee and Alabama football. Their story is a parable for how faith and football intertwine in American life, showing how even deep athletic rivalries can coexist with Christian love and commitment.

The chapter then broadens to examine how football has become a powerful force in American culture, potentially rivaling traditional religious institutions. It cites Vince Lombardi's daily prayer routine and his ability to transform biblical figures into football players through storytelling. The authors challenge skeptics who might dismiss football's theological significance, arguing that the game demands a dedication and wholehearted commitment that parallels religious devotion.

A key theme is the rise of "Global Fandom" as a new form of belonging that competes with traditional religious communities. The authors observe how sports culture has transformed various aspects of life into competitive spectacles, from cooking shows to political discourse. This shift represents a broader cultural movement where fandom provides ready-made communities and instant belonging, perhaps at the cost of deeper engagement.

The chapter concludes by positioning Christians as "gospellers on the kingdom's gridiron," suggesting that while Christ has already won the ultimate victory, believers are still called to play every down with eternal significance. This creates a theological framework that views life as a heavenly game where each person is called to be an active player rather than a passive spectator.

GAMEDAY STRATEGY

Every play and every player matters.

HALF-TIME HUDDLE— THROW A SPIRAL

 S: SPIRIT-LED STEADFASTNESS

- Mary Jameson is committed to the Tigers, and her husband Richard is committed to the Black Hawks. How does their commitment mirror steadfast faith in challenging times?

- Richard refused to speak the password "Roll Tide" to the security service one evening saying he'd rather stand watch all night than have those words pass his lips. When have you had to stand firm in your faith despite opposition?

- Professional football players have daily

rituals to prepare for game days. What can these rituals of preparation teach us about walking faithfully with God and a life designed by Jesus?

 P: Prayer

- Vince Lombardi had a practice of daily prayer before heading to the field. How might his practice inspire your own prayer life?

- How could we approach Scripture with the same intensity as football players study their playbooks?

- How can we transform a "spectator" prayer life into active conversations with God?

 I: Imagination

- How might viewing our faith journey through a football lens help us better understand biblical truths?

- How can we use sports analogies to share the gospel with others?

- How can we re-imagine our church community in an age where stadium worship often draws bigger crowds than sanctuary worship—without losing our integrity and identity?

R: Redemptive Relationships

- How do rivalries like Tennessee-Alabama challenge and strengthen our ability to love others despite differences?

- In what ways can sports bring healing and unity to divided communities?

- How might viewing ourselves as "players" rather than "fans" change our approach to church relationships?

 A: Authentic Action

- What would it look like to approach our faith with the same intensity as a football player preparing for the Super Bowl?

- How can we move from being Sunday spectators to active participants in God's mission in the world?

- What plays are God calling you to make daily?

 L: Life Story for a Living Legacy

- God highlights our kingdom-advancing efforts. How are you contributing to God's "highlight reel" through your daily chores and choices?

- What legacy are you building through your game-time decisions?

- The authors describe themselves as "gospellers"—active players rather than passive spectators. In your walk with Jesus, what would it look like for you to move from the grandstand to the playing field?

Post Game Huddle

"The cathedral of Global Christendom is being rapidly outpaced by the coliseum of Global Fandom."
~Len Sweet

- How have you observed this shift in your community?

- Is there a time when sports brought unlikely people together in your life?

- What can the church learn from these moments of connection?

Playbook Study

The playbook study provides essential terminology and concepts needed to execute the chapter's game plan effectively. Keep these formations and terms in mind as we move downfield through subsequent chapters.

Gospeller (gos·pel·er)

Historical Definition: Old English term for a follower of Jesus

Modern Application: Active participant in faith, not just a spectator

Game Usage: One who "takes the playbook to the field"

Key Play: Moving from passive belief to active engagement

Global Fandom

Formation: Modern patterns of belonging and identity

Coverage: Spans sports, entertainment, politics, culture

Defensive Weakness: Trades depth for convenience

Risk Factor: Creates passive spectators rather than active participants

AMJ (Accumulated Male Junk)

Definition: Personal collection of sports memorabilia and memories

Spiritual Parallel: Sacred remembrances and relics

Function: Connects personal story to larger narrative

Field Position: Where memory meets meaning

Cathedral of Athletics

Modern Function: Sports as sacred space

Traditional Parallel: Religious gathering places

Coverage Area: Community, ritual, shared experience

Zone Defense: Where sacred and secular intersect

House Divided

Technical Term: Mixed-sports-loyalty marriage

Strategic Value: Model for maintaining unity amid rivalry

Field Position: Where competition meets communion

Special Teams: Grace under pressure

Tale-Gate

Formation: Storytelling + traditional tailgating

Purpose: Building community through shared narrative

Field Position: Where food meets fellowship

Execution: Transforming the parking lot into a pulpit

SWEET

Blind-Side Guardian

Position: Protector of vulnerable spaces

Spiritual Application: Defending others in the faith journey

Key Skill: Change through commitment

Game Impact: Personal growth, serving others

> In football, as in life,
> your first step is the most
> important.
>
> COACH BRUCE MAYER

⚠ *Warning Signs*

Passive Spectatorship

Risk: Replacing participation with observation

Impact: Reduced spiritual growth

Counter Move: Intentional engagement

Convenient Community

Risk: Superficial connections

Impact: Lack of deep relationships

Counter Move: Intentional investment in relationships

Victory Formation

Establish credibility through authenticity.

Position sports as a lens for spiritual truth.

Introduce key themes of participation vs. spectatorship.

Set up framework for faith-sports dialogue.

Chain-Moving Challenge

This week, identify one area of your life where you've been a spectator or a referee. Take one concrete step toward active participation, whether in your faith community, family, or broader society.

> In football, as in life, your first step is the most important."
>
> COACH BRUCE MAYER

Postgame Prayer

Lord of Every Field,
You who see beyond the scoreboard and count
 victory in changed hearts,
We come before You as more than spectators in
 this grand game of life.
Transform us from bleacher-warmers into field-

SWEET

runners,
From passive observers into active gospellers.

Thank You for the sacred spaces where pigskin meets Providence,
Where underdogs find victory, and
Where divided houses discover grace.

Like a quarterback reading the defense,
Help us see the openings You provide.

Like a left tackle guarding the blind side,
Make us protectors of the vulnerable.

In a world that worships at the altar of fandom,
Remind us that our true citizenship lies in Your eternal kingdom,
Where every chain moves toward Your glory.

Grant us the strength to play through pain,
The wisdom to read Your signals,
And the courage to take the field when You call our number.

For in Your divine playbook,
Every life is a starting player,
Every day is game day, and
Every moment holds the potential for a touchdown in eternity.

In the name of the Ultimate Coach,
Who trains us in love and leads us to victory,
Amen.

PERSONAL TRAINING— CHALLENGE FLAGS

These challenges help us clarify the book's purpose—not to criticize sports or fandom, but to use football's cultural prominence as a lens for understanding and deepening faith. Like a good referee, we're not here to determine the winner but to ensure a fair and meaningful engagement between sports and spirituality.

⚠ "Isn't comparing faith to football trivializing religion?"

Referee's Ruling: Using sports as a lens to understand faith follows a rich biblical and theological tradition. The Apostle Paul frequently used athletic metaphors to explain spiritual truths (1 Corinthians 9:24–27, 2 Timothy 4:7–8). Just as Jesus used agricultural metaphors for his agrarian society, we're using sports metaphors that resonate with our sports-saturated culture.

⚠ "You admit to having limited athletic credentials. Why should we trust your sports analysis?"

Referee's Ruling: Sometimes the best observations come from those with perspective from the margins. Just as Darwin revolutionized biology as an amateur naturalist, our "nosebleed-seat" perspective offers unique insights into sports and faith. Our focus isn't on technical-game analysis but on the deeper cultural and spiritual implications of football.

⚠️ "Isn't the rise of sports fandom just harmless entertainment? Why treat it as a spiritual issue?"

Referee's Ruling: When millions more Americans watch the Super Bowl than vote in presidential elections, we're dealing with more than entertainment. Fandom has become a new form of belonging that shapes identities, values, and communities. Understanding this shift is crucial for anyone interested in how modern people find meaning and connection.

⚠️ "Are you suggesting that being a sports fan is incompatible with faith?"

Referee's Ruling: Not at all. The issue isn't sports fandom itself, but the difference between passive spectatorship and active participation in what matters most. We can enjoy sports while ensuring our deepest allegiances remain with eternal truths rather than temporary scores.

FIRST DOWN, FIRST LOVE

Coach's Corner

Challenging our assumptions often leads to deeper understanding. Don't be afraid to throw your own challenge flags as you read. That's part of the game! To get started:

- Identify areas in your life where you're just a spectator.
- Map out your "fan zones" vs. your "playing fields."
- Consider where passive observation has replaced active participation.

To train for the game:

- Start small: pick one area to move from spectator to participant.
- Build your "spiritual muscles" through daily practice.
- Find your team: connect with other "gospellers" in your community.

To make progress:

- Transform your "fandom" into active discipleship.
- Look for opportunities to bridge divided loyalties with grace.
- Practice seeing sacred moments in everyday situations.

SWEET

◉ Chain-Moving Challenge

- What is one area you've identified where you are either a spectator or a referee? _____
  _____

- What was one concrete step you took toward active participation? _____
  _____

- Notes: _____
  _____

Game II

The Divine Handoff

WHEN GOD CALLS THE PLAY

Pregame

Warmup Prayer

Divine Coach,
As we gather to explore the sacred intersections of faith and field,
Open our specs to see beyond the spectacle to the divine spectacular,
Our hearts to receive your game-changing grace, and
Our minds to understand the deeper plays you're calling in our lives.

Help us move from spectators to participants,
From fans to faithful followers,
And may our discussion spiral upward toward your glory.

SWEET

In Jesus' name,
Who turns every huddle into holy ground,
Amen.

CHAIN-MOVING CHALLENGE REFLECTION

- What was one area you identified where you had been either a spectator or a referee?
- What was one concrete step you took toward active participation?

HIGHLIGHT REEL

Game Two frames the book's central premise through a pivotal moment in USAmerican cultural history: the 1958 NFL Championship game between the Baltimore Colts and New York Giants, dubbed "The Greatest Game Ever Played." This game symbolically marks the beginning of football's gradual usurpation of Sunday's traditional role as a day reserved for church and religious observance.

This cultural shift was a "divine handoff"—the transformation of Sunday from a day of worship to one dominated by professional football. Football has become a new kind of religion, with its own rituals, devotions, and communal experiences:

- Tailgating has replaced church potlucks.
- Fantasy leagues have superseded Bible study

groups.

- "What's the score?" has become more common than "What was the sermon about?"

The chapter emphasizes that this transformation didn't happen suddenly but through a gradual process orchestrated partly by NFL Commissioner Pete Rozelle's strategic vision. The result is a profound shift in cultural priorities, with churches closing, while the NFL continues to expand its influence globally.

More than a commentary on sports or religion, this is a "two-minute drill for the soul of USAmerica's weekend." It promises to explore this cultural transformation from multiple angles, appealing to various audiences:

- Devoted Christians who also love football
- Religious people curious about football's cultural impact
- Football fans interested in the spiritual dimensions of the sport
- History enthusiasts interested in this cultural intersection

The chapter concludes by establishing the book's tone and approach. While addressing serious cultural and spiritual matters, it prom-

SWEET

ises to maintain a sense of humor and joy, comparing humor to "the Holy Spirit's Gatorade." The authors position Jesus as the "Ultimate Coach" and readers as "Most Valuable Pilgrims," setting up the sports-faith metaphors that will run throughout the book.

The overarching message is that this isn't just a book about football or religion, but rather an exploration of how these two powerful forces have shaped and continue to shape USAmerican cultural life, particularly the meaning and use of Sunday as a sacred time.

GAMEDAY STRATEGY

You don't lose ground in a single play. You lose it in a series of uncontested drives.

HALF-TIME HUDDLE— THROW A SPIRAL

 S: SPIRIT-LED STEADFASTNESS

- What can we learn from the "rookie crossing himself" about maintaining faith in pressure-filled moments?

- Where do you see examples of Spirit-led dedication in football and in faith that inspire your own walk?

- How does space shape experience?

 P: Prayer

- How might viewing prayer as a "holy huddle" change our approach to communication with God?

- What can we learn from the running back who finds "a pocket of silence" in the roaring end zone?

- How can we transform our "spectator prayers" into active engagement with God?

 I: Imagination

- How does seeing football as sacramental help us recognize God's presence in unexpected places?

- In what ways might viewing our church as a team rather than an audience change our participation?

- How can we creatively bridge the gap between stadium worship and sanctuary worship?

 R: Redemptive Relationships

- What can the post-game prayer of winners and losers teach us about unity in Christ?

- How might viewing competition through a lens of communion change our relationships?

- What lessons can we learn from the midfield embrace of opposing coaches about grace in conflict?

 A: A‍UTHENTIC A‍CTION

- How can we move from being mere fans to fellow pilgrims in our faith journey?

- What would it look like to approach our faith with the same dedication as a professional athlete?

- How can we authentically live out our faith in ways that transform "bread and circuses" into "bread of life?"

 L: L‍IFE S‍TORY FOR A L‍IVING L‍EGACY

- How are we contributing to God's story in our community beyond Sunday mornings?

- What legacy are we leaving as we navigate the path between faith and cultural influences?

- How can our personal stories of faith inspire others to move from spectators to participants in God's kingdom?

🌬️ When a play works well, you study the tape. The NFL didn't just win Sunday. It rewrote the playbook on cultural influence by understanding that people don't just need something to watch, they need something to belong to. The church's challenge isn't just about keeping people in the pews. It's about remembering that faith, like football, thrives when it creates not just converts, but community.

POSTGAME—TEAM HUDDLE

- How has your experience of Sunday changed over your lifetime? What factors influenced these changes?
- How might churches respond to competition for Sunday attention without compromising their essential message?
- What does the success of NFL Sunday suggest about human needs for community and ritual?

PLAYBOOK STUDY

Divine Handoff: The transition of Sunday's cultural significance from church to football

Cultural Usurpation: The gradual process by which one institution replaces another in social importance

SWEET

Sunday Best: The evolution of this concept from church clothes to team jerseys

Ecclesial Fumble: The church's failure to maintain its cultural position

Sacred Time: The concept of designated periods for spiritual or communal significance

🏈 Chain-Moving Challenge

This week, reflect on how football functions as a religion in your culture. What are the similarities and differences between traditional religious practice and football fandom? Choose one play strategy you can make to differentiate the two in your own life.

Postgame Prayer

Lord of Every Field,
We bow our heads before You—
Some of us still in church clothes,
Others in jersey numbers.

We recognize that You move in mysterious ways,
Even through the roar of stadium crowds and the
    quiet of empty pews.

Thank You for being bigger than our buildings,
Broader than our traditions,
And present in every gathering that brings Your

children together.

Help us see Your hand at work even as our culture changes,

Reminding us that You're not confined to sanctuaries any more than You're absent from stadiums.

Give us wisdom to read the signs of our times without losing sight of timeless truth.

Grant us the courage to face cultural change without fear,

And the insight to find You in unexpected places.

Like a good coach, help us adapt our game plan without compromising our core mission.

May we learn from both the church's fumbles and football's forward passes.

Guide us to build bridges rather than barriers between the sacred and the secular,

Remembering that all ground becomes holy when we seek Your presence there.

In the name of Jesus,
Our Ultimate Coach and Perfect Play-Caller,
Amen.

Personal Training— Fieldwork

Community Analysis

- Observe how your local community spends Sunday mornings.
- Compare attendance patterns at local churches vs. sports events.
- Note the rituals and traditions associated with both.

Personal Reflection

- Document your own Sunday routines and their evolution.
- Identify the role of both faith and football in your life.
- Consider how these influences shape your values and relationships.

Cultural Investigation

- Research local church attendance trends over the past sixty years.
- Study the growth of fantasy football participation in your area.
- Examine how local businesses adapt to Sunday football culture.

🏈 Chain-Moving Challenge

- What are some ways football functions as a religion in your current culture? _____
  _____

- What similarities and differences have you identified between traditional religious practice and football fandom? _____
  _____

- What play strategy can you implement to differentiate the two in your own life? _____
  _____

- Notes: _____
  _____

Game III

From the Sidelines to the Stars

Rediscovering Faith in a Faithless Game

Pregame

Warmup Prayer

Divine Coach,
In a world where faith seems to be playing
    defense,
Grant us the courage to run bold new plays,
The wisdom to adapt without compromising truth,
And the strength to move forward as a team.

Like Tom Dempsey, help us see beyond our
    limitations to the possibilities that arise when

SWEET

we trust in You.

May our discussion tonight reveal new ways to be both faithful and fearless in this changing game.

Through Christ, our Ultimate Victory,
Amen.

Chain-Moving Challenge Reflection

- What are some of the ways you identified that football functions as a religion in your current culture?
- What similarities and differences did you identify between traditional religious practice and football fandom?
- What play strategy did you implement in your own life to differentiate between the two?

Highlight Reel

Game Three kicks off with an examination of Christianity's current defensive position in twenty-first-century culture, particularly in regions like the Northeast and Pacific Northwest. Using football as a metaphor, it portrays Christianity as being in "prevent defense" against a culture increasingly hostile to Christian expression.

Len and Chris highlight a paradox: while Christianity

faces cultural marginalization in many spheres, the NFL remains a unique sanctuary where religious expression flourishes openly. Players like Russell Wilson, Patrick Mahomes, and Jalen Hurts freely express their faith through prayers, interviews, and even tattoos of biblical verses.

The chapter then explores several key themes:

- Media and Cultural Blindness: There's a growing "Jesus illiteracy" in elite media and cultural institutions, despite Christianity's foundational role in Western civilization's development.

- The Silencing of Faith: Religious expression has been increasingly muted in public, while the NFL's continues open to faith expressions.

- Historical Perspective: Using examples from space exploration (like Buzz Aldrin's lunar communion) to entertainment (the evolution of faith portrayal in Star Trek), the chapter traces how public expressions of faith have diminished over time.

- Corporate Culture: Commercial messaging has shifted from openly acknowledging faith (like McDonald's "get to church on time" ads) to carefully avoiding religious references altogether.

- The Power of Team: Using examples like Tom

Dempsey's record-breaking field goal and Tom Osborne's Nebraska teams, the chapter illustrates how individual uniqueness can flourish within strong team frameworks, drawing parallels to Christian community (koinonia).

The chapter concludes by celebrating the NFL's enduring legacy, tracing the evolution of legendary teams and players from the Packers of Vince Lombardi to the current Kansas City Chiefs dynasty. Throughout, it positions football as more than just a sport. It is a lens through which to view larger truths about faith, community, and human potential.

The underlying message is that while Christianity may seem to be losing ground in the broader culture, the NFL demonstrates how faith can remain vibrant and visible in public life when allowed to express itself authentically. The authors suggest that this model might offer lessons for how Christianity can navigate an increasingly post-Christian world, while maintaining its essential character and influence and even growing into a great awakening.

GAMEDAY STRATEGY

You're not playing defense in a losing game—you're on offense in an eternal victory.

FROM THE SIDELINES TO THE STARS

HALF-TIME HUDDLE— THROW A **SPIRAL**

 S: Spirit-led Steadfastness

- How can we maintain joy and steadfastness in "the ruins of our own creation?"

- What can Tom Dempsey's story teach us about persevering in faith despite obstacles?

- How might we harmonize "both contemplatives and competitors" in today's religious landscape?

 P: Prayer

- How can we develop a "muscular Christianity" in our prayer life without falling into masculine machismo or performative faith?

- What can we learn from the NFL players who openly pray on the field about authentic faith expression?

- How might we approach prayer differently if we viewed it as preparation for God's "game time?"

 I: Imagination

- How can we creatively express our faith in

a culture that increasingly views Christianity with skepticism?

- What new "playbooks" might we need to develop for sharing faith authentically in today's world?

- How can we re-imagine the church community to be more like a team pursuing a common goal?

 R: Redemptive Relationships

- How can we build authentic koinonia (spiritual team spirit) in our church community?

- What can Tom Osborne's "Move the Line Forward, Not the Ball" philosophy teach us about Christian community?

- How might we better support each other's unique gifts while maintaining unity of purpose?

 A: Authentic Action

- In what ways can we move from being spiritual "fans" to active "players" in God's mission?

- How can we demonstrate authentic faith in public spaces without retreating or becoming combative?

- What would it look like to live out "muscular Christianity" in our daily lives without the machismo and bravado?

 L: Life Story for a Living Legacy

- How can our personal faith stories contribute to a larger narrative of hope in a fragmenting world?

- What legacy are we building in terms of authentic Christian witness for future generations?

- How can we help write a new chapter of abiding presence in our current cultural moment?

For we wrestle not against flesh and blood.

EPHESIANS 6:12 (KJV)

Postgame—Coach's Corner

Game-Time Wisdom & Strategic Signals

Formation Fundamentals for SPIRAL discipleship:

1) Faith flourishes in friction.
2) Silence surrenders territory.
3) Wonder wins hearts.
4) Truth transcends trends.

Wisdom for Leaders

- Culture follows courage.
- Wonder precedes witness.
- Mystery ministers to materialism.
- Boldness builds bridges.

Wisdom for Teams

- Play offense, not defense.
- Share stories, not just statements.
- Build bridges, not bunkers.
- Transform culture through truth.

Wisdom for Disciples

- Maintain mystery in materialistic times.
- Speak truth in technical spaces.
- Find wonder in cynical places.
- Share faith in secular spaces.

The Wonder Check

- Are you marveling or managing?
- Are you witnessing or withholding?
- Are you building or bunkering?

The Cultural Connection

- Bridge, don't battle.
- Share, don't shout.
- Transform, don't retreat.

The Faith Formation

- Wonder leads to witness.
- Courage creates culture.
- Truth transforms territory.

Be strong and courageous. Do not be afraid; do not be discouraged, for the Lord your God will be with you wherever you go.

JOSHUA 1:9 [NIV]

The Final Whistle

Like the NFL players who openly share their faith, we're called to authentic expression, not anxious muteness. The early astronauts didn't leave their faith on Earth—they carried it to the stars. Your witness matters more than the world's welcome.

Chain-Moving Challenge

This week, be intentional about realizing that we're not playing defense, but we're on an eternal offensive drive—and the culture's scoreboard isn't the final word. Like astronauts seeing Earth from space, strive to see our plays through a new perspective to appreciate eternal truth.

Postgame Prayer

Divine Coach of Broken Players,
Thank You for Tom Dempsey's half foot and
> the coaches who forgot to tell him what he
> couldn't do.

Thank You for showing us that our limitations are
> often just the beginning of Your possibilities.

We confess that sometimes we've been too quiet in
> sharing our faith,
While Your spirited athletes boldly point to heaven
> after touchdowns.

Give us the courage of those NFL players who
> wear Your word on their skin and Your praise
> on their lips.

Lord, in a world where faith seems to be fading
> from public spaces—from television scripts to
> advertising jingles—
We're grateful that You're still present on any given
> Sunday,
Whether in sanctuaries or stadiums.

Thank You for those who still dare to kneel in
> prayer on national television,
Reminding us that faith needs no permission to be
> visible.

Help us remember that, like your servant Buzz
> Aldrin,

SWEET

Taking communion on the moon,
We can carry Your presence into every frontier.

Like the Steel Curtain defense working as one,
Teach us to move in perfect unity while celebrating our unique gifts.

Like Tom Osborne's Cornhuskers,
Show us how to value team above self,
Knowing that Your Spirit makes us stronger together than apart.

And Lord, as we face our own fourth-quarter deficits in this changing culture,
Remind us that the game isn't over until You say it's over.

The same Spirit that empowered Paul to run his race still empowers us today.

In the name of Jesus, who turned fishermen into world-changers,
Amen.

Personal Training— Fieldwork

The Cultural Scoreboard

- Where do you see Christianity playing defense in your community?
- When have you felt like the "visiting team" in your

own culture?

- How do you maintain faith when the crowd seems to be cheering for the other side?

The Media Blind Spot

- How has cultural Jesus-illiteracy affected your ability to share faith?
- Where do you see opportunities to bridge the gap between faith and culture?
- What "highlight reels" of faith could you share with a Jesus-illiterate world?

- **The Evangelism Formation**

- When have you gone silent when you should "go tell it on the mountain?"
- How can you share faith authentically without becoming defensive?
- Where might God be calling you to be bolder in your witness?

The Space-Faith Connection

- Like those Apollo astronauts, where have you seen God's glory in unexpected places?
- How can you maintain wonder in an age of cynicism?
- Where are you called to bridge the gap between science and faith?

SWEET

The *Star Trek* Shift

- How has cultural portrayal of faith changed in your lifetime?
- Where do you see opportunities to reintroduce wonder into sterile spaces?
- How can you maintain mystery in an age of materialism?

CHAIN-MOVING CHALLENGE

- Is it difficult to see yourself as being on an eternal offensive drive rather than playing defense? _____

- When was it hard to remember that the culture's scoreboard isn't the final word? _____

- What is one intentional thought you can keep in mind to help see your plays through a new perspective to appreciate eternal truth? _____

- Notes: _____

Game IV

Two Minute Warning

DIVINE TIMING

Pregame

Warmup Prayer

Lord of Every Moment,
As we gather to explore the intersections of time and eternity,
Help us see beyond mere spectacle to sacred participation.

Like the great cloud of witnesses surrounding us,
May we be ready to move from observers to active participants in Your story.

Transform our talk into a huddle of holy purpose,
Where each voice contributes to Your greater glory.

Through Christ, who makes every moment sacred,
Amen.

SWEET

Consider how we may spur one another on toward love and good deeds.

HEBREWS 10:24-25 [NIV]

Chain-Moving Challenge Reflection

- Was it difficult to see yourself as being on an eternal offensive drive rather than playing defense?

- Did you identify a time when it was hard to remember the culture's scoreboard isn't the final word?

- What is one intentional thought to see your plays through a new perspective to appreciate eternal truth?

Highlight Reel

Game Four centers on a pivotal moment in US cultural history: December 28, 1958, the date of "The Greatest Game Ever Played" between the Baltimore Colts and New York Giants. This game serves as a cultural watershed, marking professional football's transformation from a relatively minor sport into a dominant cultural force.

Game Four weaves several key themes:

- **Cultural Transformation:** In the 1950s, professional football ranked behind baseball, college football, horse racing, and boxing in popularity. The 1958 championship game, watched by roughly a quarter of the US population (45 million viewers), marked the beginning of football's ascendancy.

- **The Rise of a New Sunday Religion:** As football's influence grew, traditional Sunday worship began to decline. The NFL evolved from a simple sports league into a year-round cultural phenomenon with its own calendar of sacred events: combines, drafts, training camps, regular season, and playoffs.

- **Participatory Culture:** The chapter explores how the NFL mastered what scholar Edwin Schlossberg calls "interactive excellence,"creating experiences that are Experiential, Participatory, Image-rich, and Connective (EPIC). This is exemplified through the "12th Man" tradition, which began at Texas A&M and evolved into various forms of fan participation across football culture.

- **New Sacred Spaces:** The chapter examines how

sports bars have replaced traditional church fellowship halls as spaces for community gathering and shared experience. These venues serve as modern temples where fans participate in collective rituals, form tribal identities, and experience moments of transcendence together.

Game Four concludes by raising critical questions about how traditional religious institutions might learn from football's success in building community, inspiring devotion, and fostering active participation. It suggests that the church's challenge isn't just competing with football for attention, but understanding and adapting to a cultural shift where passive observation no longer satisfies people's spiritual and communal needs.

This transformation represents more than just a change in Sunday activities; it reflects a fundamental shift in how Americans experience community, meaning, and transcendence in the modern world.

Gameday Strategy

It isn't about competition between church and football, but about understanding deeper human needs for community, meaning, and participation.

Half-Time Huddle— Throw a SPIRAL

 S: Spirit-led Steadfastness

- How can we maintain spiritual steadfastness in a culture that increasingly views Sunday as game day rather than a sacred day?
- What can the "12th Man" tradition teach us about faithful readiness to serve?
- How might we cultivate the same passion for faith that football fans show to their teams?

 P: Prayer

- How can our prayer life become more participatory and less spectator-oriented?
- What can we learn from the communal energy of stadium worship that might enhance our corporate prayer?
- How might viewing ourselves as part of the "great cloud of witnesses" change our approach to prayer?

 I: Imagination

- How can we re-imagine church spaces to foster more active participation like football culture does?

- What creative ways might we engage people who seek community but find it in sports bars rather than fellowship halls?

- How can we make faith more "EPIC" (Experiential, Participatory, Image-rich, Connective) without compromising its essence?

 R: Redemptive Relationships

- How can we build deeper community connections like those formed among passionate sports fans?

- What can we learn from how football creates "tribal identity" about building authentic Christian community?

- How might we transform our church fellowship to be as engaging and participatory as a sports gathering?

 A: Authentic Action

- In what ways can we move from being passive receivers to active participants in our faith?

- How can we embody faith with the same enthusiasm and engagement that fans show at games?

- What would it look like to be as ready to

serve as E. King Gill was in the original 12th Man story?

 L: Life Story for a Living Legacy

- How can our faith communities create a lasting impact like the legendary football moments described in the chapter?

- What role do we play in writing the next chapter of Christian community in our culture?

- How can we leave a legacy of active, participatory faith for future generations?

For everything there is a season,
and a time for every purpose
under heaven.

ECCLESIASTES 3:1 (ASV)

Postgame

Coach's Corner—Field Position

The Timeline Check

- Where have your own sacred times shifted?
- What rituals have replaced traditional worship in your life?
- How has technology reshaped your spiritual rhythms?

The Cathedral Question

- Where do you find community in today's world?
- What makes an experience "EPIC" for you?
- How do you integrate spectating and participating in your faith?

The Participation Points

- When does your faith feel interactive vs. passive?
- How can worship become more experiential?
- Where might God be calling you to deeper engagement?

The Cultural Shift

- What can the church learn from football's community building?

- How might traditional faith speak to contemporary longings?
- Where has entertainment replaced enlightenment in your spiritual life?

🏁 THE FINAL WHISTLE

The NFL's success isn't just about entertainment. It's about creating meaningful participation and authentic community. The church's challenge isn't to compete with football but to rediscover its own EPIC nature.

People crave **EPIC** experiences:

E = Experiential, not theoretical or linear

P = Participatory, not passive or representational

I = Image-rich, not abstract or word-based

C = Connective, not isolated or individualistic

Wisdom for Church Leaders

- Create participation, not just presentation.
- Build a covenant community, not just a congregation.
- Offer experience, not just explanation or interpretation.
- Enable connection, not just sit-and-soak attendance.

Wisdom for Communities
- Transform spectators into participants.
- Convert audiences into actors and agents.
- Shift from passive to passionate.
- Move from watching to witnessing.

Wisdom for Individuals
- Seek engagement, not just entertainment.
- Purpose participation over performance.
- Find authentic community and engagement.
- Build meaningful connection.

Chain-Moving Challenge

This week, create EPIC moments in your faith community. Transform passive attendance into active engagement. Make every gathering an opportunity for meaningful participation.

Postgame Prayer

Lord of Sacred Time,
As we reflect on moments that change
    everything—like that December Sunday in
    1958 when television and football forever
    transformed our culture—
We pause to acknowledge Your presence in every

season and shift of history.

Father, You who turned water into wine at a
    wedding feast,
We see how You can sanctify any gathering
    Where Your children come together.

Whether in fellowship halls or sports bars,
In sanctuaries or stadiums,
You meet us where we are.

Help us remember that Your spirit isn't confined
    to traditional spaces but moves wherever two
    or three gather in authentic community.

We confess that sometimes we've been slow to
    recognize the tipping points in our lives and in
    our culture,
The moments when everything changes.

Like Johnny Unitas engineering that final drive,
Help us read the signs of our times and respond
    with wisdom and grace.

Grant us the spirit of E. King Gill—ready to step
    down from the stands and into service,
Blurring the lines between spectator and
    participant in Your kingdom work.

Let us remember that we, too, are surrounded by
    a great cloud of witnesses,
Heavenly fans cheering us on in our race of faith.

SWEET

Lord, in a world where people hunger for
>belonging, meaning, and transcendence,
Help Your church learn from both our fumbles
>and football's forward passes.

Show us how to create spaces where,
Like those first-century house churches,
People can gather to share their lives,
Their hopes, and their holy moments.

May we be neither afraid of change nor resistant to
>tradition,
But always attuned to Your Spirit's movement
>through time and culture.

Help us remember that while the games and
>gatherings may change,
You remain our Ultimate Coach in every season.

In Jesus' name,
Amen.

PERSONAL TRAINING— STRATEGIC SIGNALS

The Engagement Check

- Are you participating or spectating?
- Are you connecting or consuming?
- Are you building or merely attending?

The Community Connection

- Where do you find true fellowship?
- How do you contribute to community?
- When do you feel most connected?

The Sacred Time Survey

- What fills your Sundays?
- Where do you find meaning?
- How do you honor sacred space?

Not forsaking the assembling of ourselves together, as the manner of some is; but exhorting one another: and so much the more, as ye see the day approaching.

HEBREWS 10:25 [KJV]

Chain-Moving Challenge

- How can you create EPIC moments in your faith community? _____
_____

- When was one time this week you transformed your passive attendance into active engagement? _____

SWEET

- How can you strive to make every gathering an opportunity for meaningful participation? _____

- Notes: _____

Game V

Breaking Huddle

STEPS OF FAITH

Pregame

Warmup Prayer

Divine Coach,
As we gather in this holy huddle,
Remind us that preparation must lead to action.

Give us the courage to break formation,
To move from comfortable circles to kingdom advances.

Like quarterbacks who must trust and throw ahead,
Help us lean into Your future with bold faith.

Keep us from becoming spiritual wildebeests,

Frozen in the face of challenge.

May our discussion inspire us to move from huddle to field, from safety to service.

Through Christ, who calls us to play,
Amen.

Chain-Moving Challenge Reflection

- Did you create any EPIC moments in your faith community this week?

- Describe one time this week you transformed your passive attendance into active engagement?

- Did you make any of your gatherings an opportunity for meaningful participation?

Highlight Reel

This chapter uses the metaphor of a football huddle to examine the current state of the church and its tendency toward inward-focused, static gatherings rather than outward-focused, dynamic mission. Through the lens of football strategy and coaching wisdom, it presents several key themes:

- **The Danger of Paralysis:** Opening with Bill Walsh's warning that "quarterbacks cannot be wildebeests," the chapter draws a parallel between fatal hesitation on the field and the church's tendency to freeze in the face of cultural changes.

- **The Huddle Problem:** Using Pastor Len's circle demonstration, the chapter illustrates how churches often create ever-tighter, inward-facing circles rather than outward-facing formations ready for action. The key insight: no team ever scored from inside a huddle.

- **Forward Motion vs. Stagnation:** The chapter emphasizes that both football and faith require forward progress. It contrasts the NFL's dynamic adaptation with many churches's tendency to run "plays from 1985," highlighting the stark statistics of church decline (4,000 churches closing annually, Christian identification dropping from 77 percent to 64 percent between 2010 and 2023).

- **The EPIC Challenge:** This chapter examines how football creates Experiential, Participatory, Image-rich, and Connected communities while many churches remain stuck in passive, spectator-mode worship.

- **The Mission Imperative:** Drawing from the early church's example in Acts 8:1, where persecution was needed to scatter the apostles from their Jerusalem "huddle," the chapter argues that comfort zones must be abandoned for mission to advance.

- The chapter concludes by challenging churches

to learn from football's success in creating engaging, participatory communities rather than lamenting its cultural dominance. It poses a crucial question: When given the choice between Sunday morning services and Sunday afternoon football, why do most Americans choose the latter, and what can churches learn from this reality?

Churches must "break huddle" and move into active mission formation, or risk becoming increasingly irrelevant in contemporary culture.

Game Day Strategy

No team scores from inside the huddle. The early church didn't change the world from the upper room. They had to be scattered to spread the Gospel. Your comfort zone might be God's "delay-of-game" penalty.

Half-Time Huddle— Throw a SPIRAL

 S: Spirit-led Steadfastness

- How can we avoid becoming "wildebeests" in our faith—frozen by fear rather than moving forward?
- What makes us hesitate to break huddle in our spiritual lives?

- How can we maintain spiritual steadfastness while still being willing to innovate and adapt?

 P: Prayer

- How might our prayer life change if we viewed it as preparation for action rather than just communion?

- What can we learn from NFL quarterbacks about anticipating where God is leading rather than just reacting?

- How can we pray in ways that propel us forward rather than keeping us in comfortable circles?

 I: Imagination

- How can we re-imagine church gatherings to be more "EPIC" (Experiential, Participatory, Image-rich, Connective)?

- What would it look like to be "mobile, agile, hospitable" rather than "sterile, puerile, and senile" in our faith?

- How might we create faith communities that are as engaging as NFL game days?

 R: Redemptive Relationships

- How can we ensure our church circles face both inward and outward, like wheel spokes?

- What can we learn from football teams about balancing preparation (huddle) with action (field)?

- How might we better engage younger voices in shaping our faith communities?

 A: AUTHENTIC ACTION

- What "plays" have we been preparing for but never running in our faith life?

- How can we move from "eternal huddle" to active engagement with our mission field?

- What would it look like to be "playing to advance" rather than just protecting our territory?

 L: LIFE STORY FOR A LIVING LEGACY

- How can we ensure we're not just running "plays from 1985" in today's spiritual landscape?

- What legacy are we creating through our willingness or unwillingness to break huddle?

- How can we write new chapters of faith that will inspire future generations to move forward boldly?

For God has not given us a
spirit of fear,
but of power and of love and of
a sound mind.

2 TIMOTHY 1:7 [NKJV]

Break huddle or break impact. The choice is yours.

Postgame—Huddle Strategy

The ancients knew that some things must be stirred to come alive. The huddle is for direction, not destination. Like the early church at Pentecost, sometimes God's Spirit has to blow us out of our comfort zones. Don't confuse preparation with procrastination.

Playbook Wisdom

Wisdom for Disciples

- Your huddle shouldn't last longer than your play.
- Innovation without inspiration is just activity.
- Movement creates momentum.
- How is comfort often the enemy of our calling?

SWEET

Wisdom for Teams

- Face both ways—in for strength, out for impact.
- Turn your circle into spokes.
- Make your formation your mission.
- How can we as a team let our huddle fuel our hustle?

Wisdom for Churches

- Create EPIC moments, not just events.
- Competition isn't your enemy; complacency is.
- Learn from culture without compromising truth.
- How can we, the church, transform tradition into trajectory?

Go and make disciples of all peoples.

MATTHEW 28:19 (LIS)

CHAIN-MOVING CHALLENGE

This week, reflect on the statement: "No team scores from inside the huddle. The early church didn't change the world from the upper room. They had to be scattered to spread the Gospel."

Postgame Prayer

Divine Head Coach,
Forgive us for turning Your huddles into bunkers,
Your preparation into procrastination.

We confess that too often we've been
    wildebeests—frozen in fear—
When You've called us to be bold as lions in
    sharing Your love.

Lord, like those first apostles who needed
    persecution to scatter them from Jerusalem,
We sometimes cling too tightly to our comfort
    zones.

Break our circles open.

Turn our inward-facing formations outward.

Help us remember that while the huddle is where
    we hear Your play call,
The field is where we live it out.

Thank You for coaches like Bill Walsh who remind
    us to throw not to where people are,
But to where they're going to be.

Give us that same forward-looking vision for Your
    kingdom.

Help us anticipate where Your Spirit is moving,
Not just react to where it's been.

Give us the courage to break formation,

SWEET

To stop running plays from outdated playbooks,
To move from "mobile, agile, hostile" to "mobile, agile, hospitable."

When we're tempted to call a timeout in our comfortable circles,
Push us forward like a holy blitz into Your mission field.

Most of all, Lord, save us from the "eternal huddle."

Remind us that no team ever scored from inside a huddle,
And no church ever changed the world from inside its comfort zone.

Make us bold enough to face the opposition,
Creative enough to adapt our playbook, and
Faithful enough to keep driving toward Your eternal end zone.

In the name of Jesus, who never called a retreat,
Amen.

Personal Training— Strategic Signals

The Circle Check

- Where are you stuck in an eternal huddle?
- What "plays" has God been calling that you've

been too comfortable to run?

- When has your circle become a barrier rather than a launching pad?

The Forward Motion

- Where has comfort become a substitute for commission in your spiritual life?
- What delay-of-game penalties are you risking in God's kingdom work?
- How are you preparing for where God is sending you, not just where you are?

The Formation Focus

- Which way does your circle face—inward for comfort or outward for mission?
- What would it look like to keep one hand linked with each other while reaching out with the other hand?
- How can your community become spokes of impact rather than a closed circle?

The Magnetic Mission

- What makes your faith community compelling or repelling to outsiders?
- How does your church create EPIC (Experiential, Participatory, Image-rich, Connective) moments?

- Where might God be calling you to "call an audible" in your ministry approach?

The Game Change

- What old plays are you running that need updating for today's field?
- How can your church compete for souls without compromising its message?
- What would it take for your church to become as magnetic as a Super Bowl Sunday?

Formation Fundamentals

- Circles that face inward become stagnant.
- Comfort zones become casualty zones.
- Yesterday's playbook won't win tomorrow's game.
- Fear makes quarterbacks into wildebeests.

Chain-Moving Challenge

- How does the statement, "No team scores from inside the huddle. The early church didn't change the world from the upper room. They had to be scattered to spread the Gospel," affect you? ___

___

- How does the statement apply to you? _____

___

- Did reflecting on the statement cause you to make any intentional changes in thoughts or actions this week? _____
_____

- Notes: _____
_____

Game VI

Resilient Roots

THE ENDURING TRIUMPH OF FAITH AND FOOTBALL

Pregame

Warmup Prayer

Eternal Coach,
As we face the deep questions of faith and football,
Grant us courage to move beyond defense into divine offense,
Wisdom to navigate complex truths with grace,
And hearts ready to embrace both victory and vulnerability.

Help us see beyond temporary scorecards to the eternal game you're calling us to play.

SWEET

May our discussion honor both the risks and rewards of living faith boldly in challenging times.

Through Christ, our Ultimate Victory,
Amen.

Chain-Moving Challenge Reflection

What impact did the statement, "No team scores from inside the huddle. The early church didn't change the world from the upper room. They had to be scattered to spread the Gospel," have on you this week?

Highlight Reel

Game Six probes the resilience of Christianity and the NFL in the face of predictions of their demise.

The gravediggers have been busy. For centuries, they've been digging holes for Christianity's coffin, and more recently, they've been measuring the NFL for its burial suit. Yet both institutions stand resilient, their supposed funeral plots empty, their obituaries perpetually premature.

In 1793, when French revolutionaries rededicated Notre Dame Cathedral as a "Temple of Reason," they thought they were witnessing Christianity's last rites. Similar proclamations echoed through the halls of Soviet power, in Nietzsche's declarations, and in countless predictions of religion's imminent demise in our secular age. Yet Christianity has demonstrated a peculiar habit of turning execution grounds into gardens of renewal. The cross itself—Rome's instrument of public humiliation and death—became the very symbol of eternal life, an emblem of how this faith transforms endings into beginnings.

The NFL faces its own prophets of doom, though their predictions come armed not with philosophical arguments but with brain-scan images, domestic violence statistics, and footage of empty stadium seats during national anthems. The specters haunting America's most popular sport are both visceral and visible: former players struggling with cognitive decline, headlines of off-field violence, and the growing awareness that every bone-crushing highlight might carry a terrible hidden cost.

Dave Duerson's story haunts the league like an uneasy ghost. The former Chicago Bears safety, who won a Super Bowl and made four Pro Bowls, took his own life in 2011 with a gunshot to the chest—deliberately preserving his brain for CTE research. His final text to his family read, "Please, see that my brain is given to the NFL's brain bank." It was a dying man's effort to turn his tragedy into truth, his ending into a possible beginning for change.

Yet every Sunday, stadiums fill. Every spring, young men eagerly submit themselves to the NFL draft. The game continues, much like the faith it parallels, because both tap into something deeper than rational calculation. They offer meaning, belonging, and glimpses of transcendence that neither scientific materialism nor virtual entertainment can quite replace.

Super Bowl Sunday is no longer just a championship game but America's premier civic ritual. The halftime show has become our national cathedral service, where pop culture, patriotism, and collective identity merge in a spectacle that draws more devoted attention than any religious service. When Justin Timberlake or Lady Gaga takes that stage, they're not just performing; they're leading America's largest congregation in a celebration of its shared values and myths.

The NFL, like the church, now finds itself navigating treacherous cultural waters. Colin Kaepernick's kneeling protest forced both institutions to confront questions about justice, power, and the price of standing for principle. His exile from the league mirrors ancient stories of prophets unwelcome in their hometowns, raising uncomfortable questions about the cost of courage and the nature of true leadership.

The contrast between Pete Rozelle's visionary stewardship and Roger Goodell's reactive management of the NFL mirrors broader questions about leadership in times of crisis. Rozelle built the league into America's premier sports entertainment by understanding its role in the national psyche. Goodell's tenure has been marked by constant damage control, trying to preserve profit margins while paying lip service to player welfare—a tension familiar to any institution trying to balance mission with survival.

Yet both Christianity and the NFL endure, not because they are perfect, but because they are necessary. They provide something essential to the human spirit—community, purpose, and moments of transcendence that lift us beyond our ordinary existence. Their resilience comes not from avoiding challenges but from their capacity to absorb them, transform them, and emerge changed but unbroken.

In an age of virtual reality and digital isolation, both institutions offer something increasingly rare: authentic human drama played out in real time, with real stakes, before real communities. Whether in cathedrals or stadiums, they create spaces where strangers become family, where individual stories connect to larger narratives, and where, for a few hours at least, we can glimpse something eternal in the temporal.

Like the ancient paradox of the cross, what threatens to destroy these institutions may ultimately be what preserves them—their very human capacity to embody both triumph and tragedy, to showcase our highest aspirations and our deepest flaws, and to remind us that even in a world of endings, some things endure without end.

The chapter concludes that both institutions endure because they satisfy fundamental human needs for community, meaning, and transcendent experience, despite their flaws and challenges. Their resilience stems not from perfection but from their ability to provide something essential to the human spirit that cannot be easily replaced.

Gameday Strategy

Resilience comes not from avoiding challenges but from emerging from them, changed but unbroken.

Half-Time Huddle— Throw a SPIRAL

 S: Spirit-led Steadfastness

- How can we maintain trust and resilience in the face of predictions of Christianity's decline?

- What can we learn from football's endurance despite health concerns and controversy?
- How might we harmonize courage and wisdom in standing firm for our faith while moving forward in mission?

 P: Prayer

- How can prayer help us move from defensive to offensive positions in our faith?
- What role does preparedness play in facing life's challenges?
- How might we pray and live differently if we truly believed in "victory beyond the scoreboard?"

 I: Imagination

- How can we re-imagine church's role in society beyond just surviving cultural shifts?
- What creative ways might we engage with controversial issues while maintaining gospel integrity?
- What if we asked before every faith fight, "Did Jesus die on the cross so we can fight about this?"

R: Redemptive Relationships

- How can we build bridges across cultural divides without compromising the supremacy of Christ?

- What can we learn from football's ability to unite diverse communities?

- How might we better support those paying a high price for their faith commitments?

 A: Authentic Action

- How can we move from "playing not to lose" to "playing to win" in our faith journey?

- What would it look like to demonstrate "moral courage" rather than just "physical courage" in today's world?

- How can we take calculated risks for Christ while maintaining wisdom?

 L: Life Story for a Living Legacy

- What kind of legacy are we creating through our approach to cultural engagement?

- How can our faith communities become known more for what we're for than what we're against?

- What story will future generations tell about how we navigated these challenging times?

Postgame

⚠ Challenge Flags

- Challenge the assumption that church decline is inevitable.

    The chapter shows how Christianity has survived and thrived through numerous "death notices" throughout history.

- Contest the notion that moral courage and physical courage are the same thing.

    The chapter distinguishes between bravery in action versus standing for what's right.

- Challenge the belief that playing it safe is the best strategy.

    In both football and faith, a "prevent defense" often prevents winning.

- Dispute the idea that football's problems will lead to its demise.

    Like Christianity, football shows remarkable resilience despite predictions of its downfall.

- Challenge the assumption that protest and patriotism are mutually exclusive.

    The chapter shows how complex these intersections can be.

SWEET

Search me, O God, and know my heart;
test me and know my anxious thoughts.

PSALM 139:23 (NIV)

Chain-Moving Challenge

What steps can you take to prepare for the next time you have the tough choice to go along with the crowd or acknowledge God's leadership?

Postgame Prayer

Eternal Coach and Healer of Broken Bodies,
We pause to remember those warriors of the gridiron whose bodies now bear the cost of glory—
The ones struggling with CTE,
The ones battling daily pain,
The ones whose minds are slowly dimming.

Wrap Your healing hands around them, Lord,
And comfort their families.

We lift up the prophets of old who faced axes and persecution,

Yet kept their eyes on You.

Like that Cross that was meant to end a movement
 but instead birthed eternal life,
Remind us that what looks like defeat in Your
 kingdom often becomes victory.

Father, we confess our complex relationship with
 violence and entertainment.

Give us wisdom as we wrestle with the paradox
 of a sport we love that exacts such a terrible
 price.

Help us see beyond the spectacle to the humanity
 of each player who risks everything for our
 Sunday celebrations.

Give courage to those who must speak truth to
 power,
Whether in stadiums or sanctuaries.

Like those kneeling players who risked careers to
 stand for justice,
Help us discern when to stand, when to kneel,
 and when to speak.

May we have the wisdom to distinguish between
 physical courage and moral courage,
Between playing it safe and playing to win.

Lord of every season,
You who turned death on a cross into eternal life,

Help us remember that no institution—whether church or league—
Is beyond Your power to heal and transform.

When critics write our obituaries,
Remind us that You are the God of resurrection,
Making all things new.

In the name of Jesus,
Who faced the ultimate blitz and scored the eternal touchdown,
Amen.

Personal Training— Reality Check

The Immortality Check

- Where do you see evidence of eternal resilience in your own faith journey?

- What "obituaries" have been written about your dreams that proved premature?

- How do you distinguish between death throes and birth pangs in institutions you value?

The Violence Vector

- How do you reconcile your enjoyment of football with its human cost?

- Where in your life are you choosing entertainment over ethics?

- What price are others paying for your pleasures?

The Safety Sacrifice

- When have you prioritized success over safety in your own life?
- Where are you asking others to risk what you wouldn't risk yourself?
- How do you integrate opportunity with responsibility in guiding others?

The Cultural Crossroads

- Where do your Sunday pews meet your Sunday bleachers?
- How do you navigate between civil religion and faith religion?
- When has your faith required you to kneel while others stood—or stand while others knelt?

The Benefits Audit

- Who bears the hidden costs of your institutional loyalties?
- Where are you enjoying privileges built on others' sacrifices?
- How do you harmonize personal enjoyment with social responsibility?

The Community Question

- Which voices in your community are being silenced by the roar of the crowd?
- How do you support those broken by the systems you celebrate?
- Where might God be calling you to speak uncomfortable truth to comfortable power?

The Legacy Lane

- What price will future generations pay for today's entertainment?
- How are you preparing the next generation for better choices?
- What inheritance of justice or injustice are you passing forward?

The Prophet's Position

- Where do you stand when prophetic voice meets profitable silence?
- How do you weigh institutional loyalty with moral clarity?
- When has God called you to be both participant and critic?

🏈 CHAIN-MOVING CHALLENGE

- What steps can you take to prepare for the next time you have the tough choice to go along with the crowd or acknowledge God's leadership? _____

- Notes: _____
  _____

Game VII

Heaven's Scoreboard

MEASURING WHAT MATTERS

Pregame

Warmup Prayer

Divine Referee,
As we examine the scoreboard of our souls,
Help us measure what truly matters in Your eyes.

Like Raymond Berry questioning the field's dimensions,
Give us courage to challenge our assumptions,
Wisdom to see beyond surface victories,
And hearts ready to expand our faith's boundaries.
May our discussion help us recognize where we've been playing on fields too narrow for Your grand and glorious game.

Through Christ, who measures our hearts,
Amen.

SWEET

CHAIN-MOVING CHALLENGE REFLECTION

How did you answer: "What steps can you take to prepare for the next time you have the tough choice to go along with the crowd or acknowledge God's leadership?" Were you able to take a step?

HIGHLIGHT REEL

Game Seven delves into the complex moral territory where faith, football, and human nature intersect. Beginning with a provocative reference to "The Devil's Advocate" and Satan's claim to the twentieth century, the chapter explores how evil operates not just outside the law but often within it, challenging simplistic notions of good and evil.

Game Seven then examines football's moral ambiguity in American culture. Like the gladiatorial contests of ancient Rome, football raises uncomfortable questions about entertainment, violence, and human nature. However, the authors suggest that viewing the sport as merely "bread and circuses" misses its deeper complexity and potential for both harm and good.

This tension is illuminated through a parallel with the space race, using Martin Luther King Jr.'s critique of spending billions to reach the moon while neglecting poverty on Earth. This comparison illustrates how competing "goods" often create moral complexity, much like football's ability to simultaneously create opportunities and cause harm, to build communities and destroy bodies.

Game Seven argues that just as the space program's true value couldn't be measured solely by footprints on the moon, football's worth isn't found just in touchdowns or television contracts. Both represent complex tapestries of triumph and shortcoming, privilege and opportunity, waste and wonder. The authors suggest that Christians must learn to navigate these complexities rather than seek simple answers.

The narrative concludes powerfully with the story of Raymond Berry discovering a football field that was too narrow, using this as a metaphor for how assumptions and accepted boundaries can limit both faith and potential. This story serves as a call to question comfortable limitations and expand our vision of what's possible in both faith and life.

Throughout, the chapter maintains that while Christ has already scored the "game-winning touchdown," we live in the tension between the "already and not yet," called to discern and act wisely while recognizing that the ultimate scoreboard may show something very different from what we see in the moment.

SWEET

GAMEDAY STRATEGY

Don't get caught watching the wrong scoreboard!

HALF-TIME HUDDLE— THROW A SPIRAL

 S: SPIRIT-LED STEADFASTNESS

- How can we maintain a bedrock faith while engaging with morally complex cultural phenomena like football?

- What boundaries in our faith life need to be questioned or expanded?

- How do we discern between godly and worldly measures of success?

 P: PRAYER

- How might our prayers change if we truly believed in God's "full-sized field?"

- What keeps us praying "safe" prayers instead of mission-moving and mountain-moving ones?

- How can we develop prayer lives that challenge our comfortable boundaries?

I: IMAGINATION

- How can we re-imagine faith beyond our

self-imposed limitations?

- What might our churches look like if we measured success by God's scorecards?

- How can we envision ministry that combines both joy and justice?

 R: Redemptive Relationships

- What role does community play in expanding our spiritual boundaries?

- How might we better balance celebration with cerebration in our relationships?

- Why is it easier for us to "weep with those who weep" than to share one another's gladness, to "rejoice with those who rejoice" (Romans 12:15)?

 A: Authentic Action

- What steps can we take to expand our "field of faith?"

- How can we move beyond comfortable church roles to kingdom-advancing action?

- What spiritual risks is God calling us to take?

 L: Life Story for a Living Legacy

- What legacy are we creating through our current measurements of success?

- How can we add to a broader narrative of faith transcending cultural boundaries?
- What stories will future generations tell about how we played on God's field?

🔔 Listen up, team! You're playing on a field measured by eternity, not just your next first down. Stop running patterns based on the boundaries others have drawn for you. The field is wider, the end zone is deeper, and the game is bigger than you think. Your greatest limitation isn't the defense—it's the artificial boundaries you've accepted without measuring. Get out your spiritual tape measure and check your assumptions. Are you playing on God's full field, or are you staying safe in your comfortable narrow lanes?

Postgame—Coach's Corner

⏱ Two-Minute Drill:

Can You Read the Eternal Scoreboard? Don't get caught watching the wrong scoreboard! Here's your quick-hit summary before the clock starts:

- The game is more complex than good vs. evil.
- Evil often works within legal boundaries.
- What looks like victory on earth might be defeat in heaven.

Sometimes good competes with other good.

- Challenge the assumption that enjoyment and spirituality are opposing forces. The chapter shows how joy and justice can coexist.
- Contest the notion that evil is winning just because it appears successful. History shows God's scoreboard operates differently.

The field is bigger than you think.

- Question your accepted boundaries like Raymond Berry did.
- God's playing field is always full-sized.
- Don't let assumptions narrow your game.
- Challenge the tendency to accept spiritual boundaries without questioning them.

The ultimate victory is already secured.

- Christ scored the winning touchdown at Easter.
- We're playing in the "already but not yet."
- Satan may claim quarters, but God owns eternity.
- Dispute the idea that we must choose between celebration and service.

Keep your eyes on both scoreboards.

- Earthly success isn't always heavenly victory.

- Like the space race vs. poverty, competing goods require wisdom.
- What looks like winning might be losing, and vice versa.
- Challenge the assumption that our current field of ministry is all God has for us.

Chain-Moving Challenge

These chain-moving challenges and questions aren't about scoring points but about training hearts. Take time in the spiritual weight room this week. Sometimes the most important plays happen during practice, not the game.

How many concrete ways can you see to build bridges with those who see the "field" differently than you?

> For now we see through a glass, dimly.
>
> 1 CORINTHIANS 13:12 [LIS]

Postgame Prayer

Divine Referee of All Creation,
Give us eyes to read Your eternal scoreboard,

HEAVEN'S SCOREBOARD

Where victory and defeat often look different from what we see on our earthly fields.

Like Raymond Berry measuring that narrow field,
Grant us the wisdom and courage to question the boundaries we've accepted for too long.

Lord, in a world where good often competes with good,
Where the moon race took resources from the poor,
Where football both builds and breaks,
Help us navigate these complex moral playing fields.

Give us discernment to see beyond simple wins and losses to the deeper game You're calling us to play.

We confess that sometimes,
Like those lawyers and religious leaders Jesus challenged,
We become gatekeepers rather than gate-openers.

Forgive us when we make the field too narrow for others,
When we claim to know the final score before Your game is done.

Thank You that the ultimate touchdown has already been scored at Easter,
That we play now in the time between Your victory

SWEET

and its final revelation.

Help us remember that while Satan may claim
quarters, innings, or even centuries,
You have already won the eternal game.

Grant us the courage to question our assumptions,
To measure our accepted truths,
And to look beyond the obvious scoreboard to
Your deeper victories.

May we play on Your full field,
Not the narrow one we've drawn for ourselves.

In the name of Jesus,
Who turned the cross of defeat into history's
greatest victory,
Amen.

Personal Training— Fieldwork

Film Room of the Soul

- Where do you see yourself in today's spiritual coliseum—spectator, player, coach, or critic?

- How do you measure "success" on God's eternal scoreboard?

- When has entertainment become entrapment in your own life?

Playbook Principles

- What "whitewashed tombs" are you maintaining in your own life—areas where external appearance masks internal decay?

- Like the moon landing vs. poverty debate, where are you choosing between seemingly competing goods? How do you discern God's priorities?

- When has your joy become someone else's stumbling block?

Spiritual Status Check

- If Satan were to make his case that he "owned" your last decade, what evidence would he present? How would you counter?

- Where are you acting as a gatekeeper, potentially hindering others from accessing truth or grace?

- In what areas of your life are you allowing "legal" to substitute for "right?"

Team Formation

- How does your community unite celebration with service?

- Where might God be calling you to be both critic and participant in cultural institutions?

- How do you distinguish between righteous resistance and self-righteous rejection?

Overtime Opportunities

- What "margins" in your community are being overlooked while resources flow to more visible causes?

- When have you confused winning the game with winning the season?

- How might God be using what you consider "mere entertainment" for eternal purposes?

The Two-Minute Warning

- What play is God calling you to run when the lights are brightest?

- Where are you watching from the luxury box when God is calling you to the field?

- How will you change your game plan after today's reflections?

SIDELINE STRATEGY

Don't just run these plays solo. Take them to your small group, your family dinner table, or your prayer partner. Let them spark deep conversations that turn Monday morning quarterbacking into faith formation in the image of Christ.

HEAVEN'S SCOREBOARD

Examine yourselves to see whether you are in the faith; test yourselves.

2 CORINTHIANS 13:5 (NIV)

⚈ Chain-Moving Challenge

Sometimes the most important plays happen during practice, but not the game.

- How many concrete ways can you see to build bridges with those who see the "field" differently than you?

- Notes: _____

_____

Game VIII

The Lombardi Legacy

DISCIPLINE AS DEVOTION

Pregame

Warmup Prayer

Divine Coach,
As we study Lombardi's legacy of excellence,
Help us see discipline as a path to devotion,
Character as the foundation of victory,
And preparation as an act of worship.

May we learn to value those brief moments that
    carry eternal significance,
And like Drew Pearson, choose what's right
    Over what brings recognition.

Through Christ, who calls us to excellence,
Amen.

> For such a time as this.
>
> ESTHER 4:14 [NIV]

Chain-Moving Challenge Reflection

Sometimes the most important plays happen during practice, but not the game. How many concrete ways did you think of to build bridges with those who see the "field" differently than you?

Highlight Reel

Game Eight explores the profound legacy of Vince Lombardi, presenting him not just as a football coach but as a transformative figure who bridged the worlds of sports, spirituality, and social justice. Beginning with the concept of "Lombardi Time"—where being fifteen minutes early was considered merely on time—the chapter uses this temporal discipline as a window into Lombardi's larger philosophy of excellence and preparation.

Lombardi emerges as a study in paradox: a man whose fierce exterior masked a deeply compassionate heart, particularly evident in his unwavering stance against racial discrimination during the segregation era.

The chapter draws a compelling portrait of a leader who combined ruthless demands for excellence with an underlying spiritual foundation, demonstrated by his daily attendance at pre-dawn Mass.

The narrative then expands to explore how Lombardi's approach to coaching transcended mere sports strategy to become a comprehensive philosophy of life and leadership. His famous quote "Winning isn't everything; it's the only thing" is contextualized within a broader understanding of victory that encompassed character development and moral excellence.

The Game Eight chapter concludes with a powerful meditation on time and impact, using the striking statistic that an NFL game contains only about eleven minutes of actual play within its three-hour span. This becomes a metaphor for biblical truth: brief moments of action, properly prepared for, can have eternal significance.

This is illustrated through the story of Drew Pearson, choosing team success over personal records, exemplifying how Lombardi's values influenced not only how the game was played but also how lives were lived.

Throughout, Game Eight weaves football strategy, spiritual insight, and cultural commentary to present Lombardi as more than just a successful coach,

SWEET

but as a moral philosopher whose principles remain remarkably relevant in today's world.

His legacy is portrayed as a blueprint for combining excellence with ethics, discipline with compassion, and temporal success with eternal significance.

GAMEDAY STRATEGY

True leadership looks beyond the scoreboard to eternity.

HALF-TIME HUDDLE— THROW A SPIRAL

 S: SPIRIT-LED STEADFASTNESS

- What can Lombardi's "15 minutes early" philosophy teach us about the disciplines of faith?

- How might viewing discipline as devotion change our approach to faith?

- What does it mean to practice faith fundamentals until they become "second nature" or holy habits?

 P: PRAYER

- How can we approach prayer with the same dedication Lombardi brought to daily Mass?

- What would it mean to be on "Lombardi Time" in our devotional lives?
- How might we prepare for those brief but crucial moments when missional opportunity presents itself or greatness passes by?

 I: IMAGINATION

- How can we re-imagine discipline as a path to freedom rather than restriction?
- What would our churches look like if we applied Lombardi's standards of excellence?
- How might we better use those "eleven minutes" of crucial moments in our faith journey?

 R: REDEMPTIVE RELATIONSHIPS

- How can we harmonize high standards with grace in our relationships?
- What can we learn from Lombardi's zero-tolerance policy toward discrimination?
- What does it mean to say that faith is like learning to play any musical instrument: it takes practice?

 A: AUTHENTIC ACTION

- Discuss your "strengths inventory" or "spiritual gifts."

- How can we move from good intentions to disciplined practice?

- What would it look like to choose team (kingdom) over personal recognition?

 L: Life Story for a Living Legacy

- What kind of legacy are we creating through our daily routines and disciplines?

- How can our brief moments of trials-on-the-trail impact future generations?

- What stories will others tell about our dedication to Christ and to living a higher, sacred, sanctified life?

If you're not fifteen minutes early for heaven's appointments, you're already late for God's best.

Postgame—Preparation

Lombardi wasn't just building a football team; he was forming men. His legacy isn't measured merely in championships but in changed lives. Like Moses preparing Joshua and like Paul mentoring Timothy, Lombardi understood that true leadership looks beyond the scoreboard to eternity.

For Coaches

- Remember Lombardi's paradox: The toughest taskmaster was also the greatest advocate for his players' dignity and rights.
- Your words carry weight beyond your awareness. Use them to build up, not tear down.
- Excellence without love is just achievement; love without excellence is just sentiment.

For Teams

- Build unity through shared sacrifice, not shared comfort.
- Create standards that elevate everyone, not rules that merely restrict.
- Make room for both the Paul Hornungs and the Jimmy Taylors—different gifts serving the same mission.

For Disciples

- Show up early for God's appointments.
- Make excellence your habit, not your goal.
- Let love be your motivation, not just your method.

⚠ Challenge Flags

- Challenge the assumption that comfort and growth can coexist.

Lombardi shows that true development requires

embracing difficulty.

- Contest the notion that immediate results equal success.

The chapter demonstrates how preparation and patience create lasting impact.

- Challenge our tendency to value personal achievement over team (kingdom) success.
- Dispute the idea that those "eleven minutes" of actual play are all that matters.

The preparation and discipline between moments are crucial.

- Challenge the belief that spiritual growth happens without intentional, consistent practice.

Analysis

The Lombardi Mirror

- Where have you confused winning with worth?
- How are you building character through challenge?
- When has your passion for excellence overshadowed your practice of grace?

The Legacy Check

- What will those who follow remember about your leadership?

- How are you advocating for those without voice or power?
- Where are you building bridges while others build walls?

> Whatever you do, work at it with all your heart, as working for the Lord, not for human masters.
>
> COLOSSIANS 3:23 (NIV)

Chain-Moving Challenge

This week, consider your leadership style.

- Does your style reflect your position, your caring, your planning, your purpose, or something else?
- Are your leadership goals focused more on the scoreboard or on eternity?
- Do you have different leadership styles for different parts of your life? Is this a good thing?
- Why or why not?

Postgame Prayer

Lord of Lombardi Time,
Thank You for those who teach us that being early

SWEET

>isn't just about punctuality,

But about preparation for Your purposes.

Like Coach Lombardi kneeling in pre-dawn Mass,
Help us find our strength in quiet moments
>With You before the day's battles begin.

We're humbled by the paradox of Your servants—
>like Lombardi, whose iron fist carried a velvet heart,

Who demanded excellence while defending equality,

Who could strike fear with a glare yet stand fearlessly against injustice.

Remind us that Your strength is made perfect in such holy contradictions.

Thank You for those eleven precious minutes of actual play in a three-hour game.

Help us see in this Your deeper truth—that our brief moments of faithful action flow from hours of preparation in Your presence.

Like Drew Pearson choosing team over personal glory,
Give us the wisdom to see beyond statistics to significance.

Father, in a world obsessed with comfort,
Remind us of Lombardi's gospel of effort,
That excellence isn't just encouraged but expected.

When we're tempted to take the easy route,
To drop out of life's hard plays like those six players leaving the huddle,
Steel our spirits for the longer road.

Most of all, Lord, help us remember that, like every practice on Lombardi's field,
Each moment of our lives is sacred ground for Christ formation.

May we treat every day, every task, and every encounter is an opportunity to live and glorify You.

In the name of Jesus, our Ultimate Coach,
Amen.

Personal Training— Practice Field Principles

Time Management

- Fifteen minutes early is on time.
- On time is late.
- Late is unacceptable.
- God's timing is perfect.

Character Formation

- Excellence is a habit.
- Discipline is freedom.

- Character precedes achievement.
- Service surpasses success.

Leadership Lessons

- Love drives excellence.
- Standards elevate everyone.
- Justice requires courage.
- Unity transcends uniformity.

Training Strategies

When Time Meets Eternity on Lombardi Time

Excellence isn't about perfection; it's about persistence. Character isn't formed in comfort but in challenge. Leadership isn't about position but purpose and stepping up to your "Esther" moment.

Time and Preparation

- Where in your life are you living on "Lombardi Time," and where are you running late or barely on time for God's appointments?
- How might being fifteen minutes early change your spiritual formation?
- How might treating time as sacred change your daily rhythms?

Excellence and Grace

- How do you weigh the pursuit of excellence with the reality of grace?
- When has God used your failures to teach you about God's perfection?
- Where might you be "cheating the Lord" by not using your gifts to their fullest?

Community and Character

- How does your community shape your character, for better or worse?
- Where are you called to be a Lombardi-like voice for justice and equality?
- How can you build team unity without compromising standards?

Heart Power and Hard Truth

- When has tough love helped shape your faith formation?
- How do you dovetail compassion with accountability in leadership?
- Where might God be calling you to speak the hard truth in love?
- What talents are you burying instead of investing?
- Where has God gifted you that you're holding back?

- How are you using your position to advocate for others?

> "I don't know, I don't care, and it doesn't matter" will be the final human prayer.
>
> JACK KEROUAC,
> DESOLATION ANGELS (1965)[1]

Reflection

On Daily Mass and Daily Practice: Legacy and Light

- What daily practices are you developing that will outlive you?
- How are you translating eternal truths for a new generation?
- Where is God calling you to be both fedora and collar, both coach and priest?
- What daily disciplines shape your life of faith?
- Where have you substituted activity for intimacy with God?
- How does your private devotion fuel your public performance?

---

1. With thanks to Terry Rankin for finding for me this quote.

Tell of your "Esther Moments" when you had to face:

(Note: If you're not familiar with the story of Esther, you may want to take time to read this Old Testament book in the Bible.)

- A personal crossroads where you had to decide whether to step into God's mission for your life
- A time when you must choose between personal safety and taking a bold stand for others
- The moment of accepting a calling or responsibility that carries significant risk
- The transformation from a passive position of privilege to active advocacy

Chain-Moving Challenge

- What is your leadership style? _____

- What does your leadership style reflect? _____

- Are your leadership goals focused more on the scoreboard or on eternity? _____

- Do you have different leadership styles for different parts of your life? Is this a good thing? Why or

SWEET

why not? _____

_____

• Notes: _____

_____

Game IX

THE BELICHICK BLUEPRINT

STRATEGY AND SPIRIT

PREGAME

WARMUP PRAYER

Divine Strategist,
As we explore the complex intersection of excellence and integrity,
Help us see beyond surface victories
To the deeper game You're calling us to play.

Grant us wisdom to adapt like Belichick,
Courage to stand firm like Lombardi, and
Hearts that seek Your approval above the world's scoreboard.

Through Christ, our Ultimate Coach,
Amen.

Chain-Moving Challenge Reflection

- Did you learn anything surprising about your leadership style?
- Did you decide to make any changes to your leadership style based on what you learned?

Highlight Reel

Game Nine presents Bill Belichick as a complex figure of almost biblical proportions, exploring his journey from football apprentice to controversial legend through the lens of theology and prophetic narratives. Beginning with young Belichick's *lectio-divina*-like study of game film under his father's tutelage, the chapter traces his evolution through moments of both triumph and tribulation.

The narrative weaves through several key periods: his wilderness years in Cleveland, his apprenticeship under Bill Parcells with the Giants, and his eventual rise to prominence with the New England Patriots. The chapter gives particular attention to the Brady-Belichick partnership, likening it to a covenant relationship that transformed a mediocre franchise into a dynasty.

A central focus is placed on Super Bowl LI's miraculous 28–3 comeback against the Atlanta Falcons, presented as a parable of resurrection and persistence. This is contrasted with darker moments like the Spygate scandal and the mysterious Butler benching in Super Bowl LII, exploring how success can breed both glory and temptation.

The chapter concludes with a detailed examination of the six camps of Belichick criticism, using these perspectives to illuminate deeper truths about leadership, excellence, and the price of greatness. A final comparison with Vince Lombardi shows how different paths can lead to similar destinations in the pursuit of excellence, while raising essential questions about the relationship between winning and virtue.

Throughout, the chapter uses religious metaphors and biblical parallels to explore larger themes about human nature, leadership, and the complex relationship between success and integrity. The narrative suggests that Belichick's story, like all great leadership tales, contains both light and shadow, triumph and transgression, offering lessons that transcend football to touch on universal truths about the human condition.

SWEET

GAMEDAY STRATEGY

Your legacy isn't just what you achieve but who you become and who you help others become.

HALF-TIME HUDDLE— THROW A SPIRAL

 S: Spirit-led Steadfastness

- What are the hidden costs of conflating professional accomplishment with growth in grace and faith?

- How can we distinguish between healthy ambition and ego-driven striving? Do you agree that "EGO" can be an acronym for "Edging God Out."

- What can we learn from Belichick's adaptability in our journey of faith?

- How do we combine flexibility in methods with firmness in message?

 P: Prayer

- How might viewing God as our "Head Coach" change our prayer life?

- What can we learn from Belichick's preparation habits about spiritual readiness?

- How do we pray through seasons when God's "game plan" seems thick and foggy?

 I: Imagination

- How do we unlock the transformative potential of daily practices of faith in unconventional settings? What happens when we re-imagine our faith traditions as a source of creative disruption rather than just personal salvation and shalom?

- What might it look like to adapt our ministry approaches while maintaining core truth?

- How can we better see value in overlooked people and undervalued opportunities?

 R: Redemptive Relationships

- How do we maintain team (community) focus over individual success?

- What can we learn from Belichick's "Do Your Job" philosophy about serving others?

- How might we better support each other through both victories and controversies?

 A: Authentic Action

- How can we pursue excellence without compromising integrity?

- What does it mean to "fight for inches" in our living out the faith?
- How do we respond when facing our own "Super Bowl LI" moments of seeming defeat?

 L: Life Story for a Living Legacy

- What kind of legacy are we creating through our daily choices?
- How can our response to criticism shape our witness?
- What story will future generations tell about your sacred quest and your pilgrimage toward truth?

Postgame—Coach's Corner

These thoughts and questions probe the dynamics of victory-meeting-vulnerability. So keep prodding and pricking and priming the conversation.

The 28–3 Moment: Divine Comebacks

- God specializes in impossible situations. When Israel stood at the Red Sea, when David faced Goliath, when Jesus lay in the tomb—these were all 28–3 moments.
- Don't judge the game at halftime. Heaven's clock

runs differently than ours.

Strategic Formation

- What is your current "impossible" situation?
- List past victories that seemed impossible.
- Document daily progress, no matter how small.
- Keep your eyes on the eternal scoreboard, not the current situation.
- **The Excellence Equation**
- Success without integrity is just achievement; integrity without excellence is just intention.
- Jesus calls us to be "wise as serpents and innocent as doves"—living with excellence that doesn't compromise integrity and wisdom that doesn't sacrifice witness.

Game Plan

- Define success by eternal standards.
- Measure progress by faithfulness, not just results.
- Let your methods match your message.
- Character is the ultimate scoreboard; narratives over numbers; stories over statistics.

The Solitude Season

- Leadership can be lonely, but it's supposed to be. Moses had his mountain, Jesus had His desert,

Paul had his Arabia. These weren't punishments but preparations.

- When success isolates you, you're in good company.

Formation Drills

- Build your prayer tent like Moses.
- Seek your Gethsemane moments.
- Find your upper room companions.
- Solitude with God beats popularity with crowds.

The Critics' Corner

- Criticism often confirms calling. Noah faced mockers while building the ark. Nehemiah rebuilt the walls under threat. Jesus faced constant criticism from religious leaders.
- Opposition doesn't mean you're wrong—sometimes it means you're right.

Defensive Strategy

- Filter criticism through prayer.
- Learn from your opponents.
- Let opposition refine your mission.
- Critics can be unwitting prophets.

The Innovation Integration

- Tradition keeps us grounded; innovation keeps

us growing. Like Jesus teaching "you have heard it said … but I tell you," we must honor the past while embracing God's future.

- Not everything old is holy, and not everything new is heresy.

Playbook Principles

- Root innovation in eternal truth.
- Test new, timely methods against timeless principles.
- Let tradition inform but not imprison.
- Live out of the past, not in the past.

God makes all things new, not all new things.

The Success Spectrum

- Success in God's kingdom often looks like failure to the world. The cross seemed like defeat until Sunday morning.
- Your current struggle might be preparation for your greatest victory.

Victory Formation

- Define success by obedience, not outcomes.
- Measure achievement by eternal impact.
- Count the cost before the commitment.
- God's foolishness is wiser than human wisdom.

SWEET

◉ Chain-Moving Challenge

Your legacy isn't just what you achieve but about who you become and who you help others become. This week, consider: What does your legacy currently look like? Who are you helping as part of your legacy?

Postgame Prayer

Divine Mentor of Both Prophets and Prodigals,
Like young Belichick, studying game film at his father's feet,
Teach us to seek wisdom in daily discipline.

Help us remember that greatness often begins in quiet rooms,
Poring over life's sacred stories with patient hearts.

Lord, we've seen in Belichick's story how the wilderness years in Cleveland prepared him for future glory.

When we face our own seasons of setback and seeming failure,
Remind us that You often use such times to shape us for purposes we cannot yet see.

Thank You for moments of resurrection like that 28–3 comeback,
Showing us that no deficit is too deep for Your

redemptive power.

Help us remember that life, like football, is often won in inches—that persistence itself can be a form of prayer.

Forgive us, Father, when, like Belichick in Spygate,
Success tempts us to compromise our integrity.

Remind us that true victory isn't just about the score,
But about how we play the game.

When we face our own Butler-benching moments—times of inexplicable loss or confusing decisions—
Give us grace to trust Your larger purpose.

Most of all, Lord, help us remember that like both Lombardi and Belichick,
There are many paths to excellence but only one path to true greatness—
The path of integrity before You.

May we pursue victory in ways that honor both the game and its divine Maker.

In Jesus' name—who turned the cross of defeat into history's greatest victory,
Amen.

Personal Training— Film Study

Several biblical figures learned from their fathers or mentors in ways that parallel Belichick's apprenticeship. Perhaps Timothy is the closest parallel since we actually have scriptural evidence of his early learning. Here are five stories for further study:

1) Timothy—one of Paul's much-loved missionary partners—learned from both his mother, Eunice, and grandmother, Lois, from childhood (2 Timothy 1:5, 3:15) and later under Paul's mentorship. Paul refers to him as "my true son in the faith" (1 Timothy 1:2).

2) Solomon learned from his father, King David, who specifically instructed him about building the temple and ruling wisely (1 Chronicles 28:9–10, 1 Kings 2:1–9).

3) Joshua served as Moses's aide (Exodus 24:13, 33:11) before becoming his successor, leading the people into the Promised Land, and winning many battles.

4) Samuel, the son of Hannah, who gave him to the Lord, learned under Eli in the temple from childhood, though Eli was his mentor rather than his father (1 Samuel 3).

5) Elisha learned under the mighty prophet Elijah, though again this was a mentor relationship rather than father-son (1 Kings 19:19–21).

Coaching Clipboard: Quick Hits for the Heart

On Impossible Odds

- Your Red Sea moment is God's highlight reel opportunity.
- Don't confuse God's silence with His absence.
- The bigger the deficit, the greater the testimony.

On Excellence

- Integrity is not negotiable.
- Excellence honors God; perfectionism denies God.
- Your methods preach louder than your message.

On Criticism

- Opposition often confirms direction.
- Critics can't cancel calling.
- Let persecution perfect your purpose.
- "Disrespect is a gift." ~Tom Brady

On Innovation

- Honor the past; embrace the future.
- Tradition is a guide, not a guard.

SWEET

- Methods change; message remains.

Sideline Strategy

Don't just survive life's challenges—leverage them.

Let isolation deepen your dependence on God.

Let criticism sharpen your mission.

Let impossible odds showcase God's power.

Victory Vision

Success isn't measured by temporal scoreboards but by eternal impact. You're not running a sprint, but you're not running a marathon either. You're running a relay. Your legacy isn't just what you achieve but who you become and who you help others become, with "others" defined in terms of time as well as in space.

> Not that I have already obtained all this, or have already arrived at my goal, but I press on to take hold of that for which Christ Jesus took hold of me.
>
> PHILIPPIANS 3:12 [NIV]

THE BELICHICK BLUEPRINT

🏈 Chain-Moving Challenge

Your legacy isn't just what you achieve but who you become and who you help others become. This week, consider your legacy:

- What does your legacy currently look like? ____
  _____
- Who are you helping as part of your legacy? ____
  _____
- Notes: _____
  _____

Game X

Crossing the Goal Line

WHERE HEAVEN MEETS EARTH

Pregame

Warmup Prayer

Eternal Coach,
As we gather at this intersection where heaven meets earth,
Help us see the sacred in each moment,
From shattered dreams to unexpected grace.

Like John Madden finding new purpose,
May we recognize Your redirecting hand.

Guide us to choose the fuel that builds up,
And tune our hearts to Your divine frequency.

Through Christ, who crosses every goal line with us, Amen.

Chain-Moving Challenge Reflection

This week, we looked at how our legacy is not only what we achieve but also who we become and who we help others become.

- Were you able to identify what your legacy currently looks like?
- Are you helping someone else become a better legacy?
- Did you make any decisions based on the answers to these questions?

Highlight Reel

Game Ten uses John Madden's remarkable career trajectory to explore themes of divine purpose working through apparent setbacks and the power of adaptation in both football and faith. Beginning with what seemed like tragedy—a career-ending knee injury in the 1958 Philadelphia Eagles training camp—the chapter shows how this apparent ending became the foundation for Madden's extraordinary legacy.

The narrative unfolds in three distinct acts. First is the "Blessed Injury," where Madden's misfortune leads to crucial mentorship from quarterback Norm Van Brocklin, who teaches him the art of film study. This section illustrates how divine purpose often works through apparent defeats, turning obstacles into opportunities.

The second act covers Madden's coaching career with the Raiders, where at age thirty-two, he became head coach and established a remarkable .763 winning percentage. This period demonstrates how his earlier setback prepared him for greater success, as he built a unique culture around three simple commandments: be on time, pay attention, and when called upon, play like hell.

The third and final act explores Madden's evolution from coach to broadcaster to video game pioneer, showing how each transformation reached increasingly larger audiences while maintaining his core principles. This progression serves as a parable for how traditional institutions might adapt their methods while preserving their message.

Throughout, the chapter draws parallels between Madden's journey and biblical narratives of transfiguration, using his story to explore larger themes about divine adaptation, sacred reinvention, and spiritual innovation. It concludes with a medita-

SWEET

tion on the nature of rivalry and competition in both sports and faith, challenging readers to consider how to maintain grace while pursuing excellence.

Game Ten's central message is that God often works through unexpected channels and apparent setbacks to achieve greater purposes, using Madden's multifaceted career as a template for understanding how traditional truths can speak through new methods to reach new generations.

GAMEDAY STRATEGY

Success is not final, failure is not fatal: it is the courage to continue that counts.

HALF-TIME HUDDLE— THROW A SPIRAL

 S: SPIRIT-LED STEADFASTNESS

- How do we maintain faith when apparent endings become divine beginnings?

- What can we learn from Madden's journey about adapting to God's unexpected plans?

- Where has God gifted you extraordinarily? How do you steward those gifts?

P: Prayer

- How might viewing setbacks as divine classrooms change our prayer life?
- What role does contemplative silence play in tuning our hearts to God's frequency?
- How has your wounding become your witness?

 I: Imagination

- How can we create more resonant and welcoming sacred spaces?
- Where might you be trying to recreate past glory instead of seeking a new vision?
- What perfect moments are you grateful for without needing to repeat?

 R: Redemptive Relationships

- What can we learn from the Bears' story about maintaining unity in success?
- How do we balance grace and accountability in helping others, like Parcells did with Taylor?
- How do you love difficult people without endorsing their choices?

 A: Authentic Action

- What practical steps can we take to create

more EPIC (Experiential, Participatory, Image-rich, Connective) faith communities?

- Like the Bears' front office, where have short-term decisions created long-term consequences?

- When has frugality cost more than spending would have?

 L: Life Story for a Living Legacy

- Where has worldly success threatened your missional focus? When has success itself become your greatest enemy?

- How do you maintain hunger after achieving your goals?

- What "Super Bowl Shuffles" have distracted you from your core mission?

Sometimes God gives us one perfect season to show us what's possible, not what's sustainable. The question isn't whether you can recreate yesterday's miracle, but whether you're ready for tomorrow's.

POSTGAME

PLAYBOOK—FORMATION FUNDAMENTALS

- Every setback contains a seed of comeback.
- Transitions are training grounds.
- Innovation is a spiritual discipline.
- Adaptation is an act of faith.

COACH'S CORNER—GAME PREP

In football, as in faith, it's not about how often you get knocked down. It's about how many times you get back up and find new ways to move forward. "Not that I have already obtained all this, or have already arrived at my goal, but I press on to take hold of that for which Christ Jesus took hold of me" (Philippians 3:12 NIV)." Or in a current life-mantra, "Success is not final, failure is not fatal: it is the courage to continue that counts."

The Door Check

- What doors have closed in your life that led to unexpected openings?
- Where are you stuck, staring at a closed door instead of seeking new opportunities?
- How has failure prepared you for future success?

The Adaptation Audit

- When have your plans been divinely interrupted?
- How have your setbacks become setups for something greater?
- Where might God be calling you to reinvent yourself?

The Mentorship Mirror

- Who has been your "Norm Van Brocklin," teaching you during your injury time?
- Where are you called to be a mentor to others in transition?
- How do you recognize divine appointments in unexpected places?

The Innovation Investigation

- What new "languages" is God calling you to learn?
- How can you translate eternal truth into contemporary contexts?
- Could technology be your next mission field?

Wisdom

For Leaders

- Love the person before the performance.
- Set standards without setting traps.

- Create space for redemption.
- Hold truth and grace in tension.

For Teams
- Support without enabling.
- Challenge without condemning.
- Celebrate gifts while addressing gaps.
- Build accountability through relationship.

For Personal Growth
- Recognize gift isn't character.
- Transform pain into purpose.
- Use influence for impact.
- Stand in grace without presuming upon it.

Like Taylor on that pain-filled day in New Orleans, our greatest testimony often comes through our deepest struggles. The same God who gives extraordinary gifts also provides extraordinary grace—not to excuse our failings, but to transform them.

Sacred Strategy

- Celebrate the moment without trying to clone it.
- Learn from glory without being enslaved to it.
- Stay hungry for new miracles.
- Keep your eyes on eternal touchdowns.

SWEET

Yet know this: God's plans for tomorrow might look nothing like God's victories of yesterday.

Chain-Moving Challenge

This week, learn and apply Madden's three rules for your life story and faith journey:

- Rule #1: Be on time for God's appointments.
- Rule #2: Pay attention to divine direction.
- Rule #3: Move with holy boldness when called.

Being confident of this very thing,
that he which hath begun a good
work in you will perform it until
the day of Jesus Christ.

PHILIPPIANS 1:6 [KJV]

Postgame Prayer

Divine Coach of Second Chances,
Like John Madden lying on that Eagles' training
    table with a shattered knee and shattered
    dreams,
We often can't see how You're working behind our
    apparent losses.

Thank You for the Van Brocklins in our lives—
   those unexpected mentors who help us see
   opportunity in our obstacles.

Lord, we confess that sometimes we resist change,
Clinging to our original game plans instead of
   trusting Your larger purpose.

Help us remember that, like Madden moving
   From field to booth to digital realm,
Your calling evolves but never ends.

Each transformation isn't a departure from
   purpose but a deeper dive into Your divine design.

Thank You for showing us through Madden's story
   that every closed door hides an open one,
That today's setback might be tomorrow's setup.

When we face our own training room moments,
Help us stop asking "Why me?" and start asking
   "What next?"

Give us the wisdom to see beyond current battles
   to eternal purposes,
The courage to let competition make us better
   Without making us bitter.

Remind us that, like Madden crashing the Hogs'
   party,
True fellowship can transcend rivalry.

Most of all, Lord, help us remember that You

specialize in turning endings into new beginnings.

May we, like Madden, be willing to adapt our methods while maintaining our message,
Always ready to bring Your truth to new generations in ways they can hear and understand.

In the name of Jesus,
The ultimate Game-Changer,
Amen.

Personal Training— Coach's Corner

The Wonder Working

Your current crisis is God's classroom for your next calling. As Helen Keller noted, "When one door closes, another opens." But as anyone who has wandered the hallways of transition knows, those in-between times test our faith the most. Or as motivational speakers like to put it, "the hallway can be hell." Just ask David, who waited years between his anointing and his throne.

Not every victory needs to become a dynasty. Sometimes God's purpose is fulfilled in a single perfect season, a moment of glory that points to greater truths. The challenge isn't recreating past success but remaining open to new miracles.

Instant Replay

Learning from Fantasy Football, we see an EPIC Framework. Read through the following EPIC components. What would you add? What would you subtract?

E—Experience is Essential

People seek meaningful participation.

Details matter in creating engagement.

Community forms around shared passion.

Investment follows interest.

P—Participation Matters

People want to be players, not spectators.

Analysis deepens engagement.

Community requires interaction.

Investment creates commitment.

I—Image-rich Engagement

Visual storytelling drives connection.

Stats become compelling narratives.

Player photos humanize the experience.

Graphics make data memorable.

Live scoring creates dramatic tension.

Team logos build identity.

Color schemes trigger emotional investment.

Visual updates create anticipation.

Player cards become trading icons.

Fantasy platforms offer rich visual interfaces.

Rankings and standings tell visual stories.

Victory animations celebrate achievement.

C—Connection is Key

Daily engagement beats weekly meetings.

Shared activities build relationships.

Competition can strengthen community.

Technology can enhance tradition

Here is a sacred application of the EPIC interface. To make the church EPIC would mean the following:

Experiential—from passive to passionate

Transform sermons into stories.

Convert lessons into life changes.

Turn worship into wonder.

Participatory—from audience to actors

Make every member a minister.

Turn listeners into leaders.

Transform spectators into servants.

Image-rich—from words to wonder

Use visual storytelling in teaching.

Create meaningful symbols for ministry.

Design spaces that tell stories.

Develop a visual language for faith.

Make Scripture visually accessible.

Create memorable ministry moments.

Use technology to enhance, not replace.

Let architecture amplify messages.

Design services with visual flow.

Create shareable faith moments.

Connective—from weekly to walking together

Build digital bridges between Sundays.

Create ongoing conversation.

Foster authentic community.

What do you think of the following conclusion? When the church becomes as EPIC as fantasy football:

- We won't compete with culture; we'll create it.
- We won't chase relevance; we'll define it.
- We won't seek transfiguration; we'll embody it.
- We won't describe a different world; we'll birth it.

SWEET

Strategic Signals

The Transition Check

- Are you waiting or wasting?
- Are you learning or lamenting?
- Are you adapting or avoiding?

The Innovation Inventory

- What new methods await?
- What doors are opening?
- What skills need developing?

The Legacy Look

- How will your story inspire?
- What wisdom can you share?
- Where might God use your experience?

Sideline Strategies

The Daily Discipline

- Study like Van Brocklin.
- Lead like Madden.
- Adapt like Paul.
- Innovate like Joseph.

The Growth Game Plan

- Learn from closed doors.

- Listen in hallways.
- Look for new openings.
- Leap when called.

> Therefore, there is now no condemnation
> for those who are in Christ Jesus.
>
> ROMANS 8:1 [NIV]

Chain-Moving Challenge

How has applying Madden's three rules for your life story and faith journey impacted your week?

- Rule #1: Be on time for God's appointments. ___

- Rule #2: Pay attention to divine direction. ___

- Rule #3: Move with holy boldness when called.

- Notes: ___

Forget the former things; do not dwell on the past. See, I am doing a new thing!

ISAIAH 43:18-19 (NIV)

Game XI

Red Zone Redemption

FROM FUMBLES TO FAITH

Pregame

Warmup Prayer

Divine Coach,
As we explore stories of redemption and grace,
Open our hearts to see victories beyond the scoreboard,
Touchdowns that matter in eternity, and
Plays that transform lives through love.

Help us recognize opportunities to advance Your kingdom,
Not just from the sidelines, but in the game itself.

Through Christ, who makes every redemption possible,
Amen.

SWEET

CHAIN-MOVING CHALLENGE REFLECTION

Last week, we learned and applied Madden's three rules for our life stories and faith journeys. What impacts did these rules have on your life?

- Rule #1: Be on time for God's appointments.
- Rule #2: Pay attention to divine direction.
- Rule #3: Move with holy boldness when called.

HIGHLIGHT REEL

The chapter opens by contrasting how modern politics, like football, has abandoned the moderate middle for end-zone extremes. It then pivots to explore how heaven celebrates spiritual victories more intensely than any Super Bowl moment, particularly when souls turn toward home. The text challenges believers to move from spiritual spectating to active participation in God's game plan.

The Pittsburgh Steelers of the 1970s serve as a prime example of faith and football mixing successfully. While their rivals, the Oakland Raiders, celebrated breaking rules, the Steelers broke stereotypes about faith and football being incompatible. Their locker room became a place where Bible study replaced trash talk and prayer warriors wore Super Bowl rings.

Tony Dungy emerges as a central figure, representing a Christ-centered approach to leadership dubbed the "Dungy Way." His story demonstrates how one can:

- Win without yelling.
- Succeed without compromising values.
- Lead through quiet strength.
- Prioritize family and faith over football.
- Transform lives through prison ministry.

The second half of the chapter explores three powerful narratives of redemption:

1) Ernie Holmes' Story, from a violent breakdown on a Pennsylvania highway to redemption:

- Demonstrates how grace outscores justice
- Shows the power of second chances through:
  - Law enforcement's restraint
  - The Rooney family's investment in his recovery
  - Community support for his transformation
  - Becoming a Baptist minister after his NFL career

2) Fran Tarkenton's "Broken Pattern" Principle:

- Illustrates how God transforms broken plays into opportunities
- Shows divine creativity in redeeming shattered

SWEET

situations

- Demonstrates how setbacks become setups for God's grace

3) Warrick Dunn's Journey:

- Lost his mother to violence as a teenager
- Found family through Tony and Lauren Dungy
- Chose forgiveness over revenge
- Transformed tragedy into ministry through the "Homes for the Holidays" program
- Demonstrates how pain can birth purpose

The chapter emphasizes several key game-winning insights. Here are three of them.

1) True Victory Goes Beyond the Scoreboard:

- Heaven celebrates transformed lives more than touchdowns.
- Real success means investing in eternal outcomes.
- Every act of grace scores points in heaven's playbook.

2) Redemption Has No Limits:

- No one is beyond grace's reach.
- Mercy scores more than judgment.
- Investment in broken lives pays eternal dividends.

- You can't out-love the Lord.

3) Transfiguration Through Grace:

- God specializes in redeeming the seemingly irredeemable.
- Pain can become purpose.
- Forgiveness gains more yards than grievance.

Final Score: The chapter concludes by emphasizing that while earthly records celebrate athletic achievements, heaven's highlight reel features different victories:

- Each time forgiveness defeats bitterness
- Every moment grace transforms a life
- All instances where tragedy becomes blessing

The ultimate message is that we're all called to move from the comfortable sidelines into the game of eternal consequence, where true victories are measured not in points scored but in lives healed and made whole through grace and redemption.

Gameday Strategy

In God's playbook, the greatest plays often come from our deepest pain, and the most meaningful touchdowns are scored in the end zone of grace.

SWEET

HALF-TIME HUDDLE— THROW A **SPIRAL**

 S: SPIRIT-LED STEADFASTNESS

- What can we learn from Tony Dungy about staying faithful in both victory and loss?

- How do we maintain spiritual steadiness when facing our own "red zone" moments?

- What does it mean to score "touchdowns in eternity?"

 P: PRAYER

- How might viewing prayer as heaven's celebration change our approach to intercession?

- What can we learn from Warrick Dunn about praying through pain toward purpose?

- How do we pray for those who seem beyond redemption, like Ernie Holmes once was?

 I: IMAGINATION

- How can we re-imagine our failures as opportunities for God's grace?

- What would our churches look like if we celebrated spiritual victories like touchdown moments?

- How might we better envision grace's power to transform lives?

 R: Redemptive Relationships

- How can we better support those going through their own "broken patterns?"
- What can we learn from the Steelers about creating communities of grace?
- How might we move from being spiritual spectators to active participants in others' redemption?

 A: Authentic Action

- What does it mean to choose forgiveness over revenge in practical terms?
- How can we create "Homes for the Holidays" moments in our own spheres of influence?
- What steps can we take to move from the sidelines into the game of eternal consequence?

 L: Life Story for a Living Legacy

- What kind of spiritual touchdowns are we scoring that will echo in eternity?
- How can our redemption stories inspire hope in others?
- What legacy of grace are we creating through our responses to life's challenges?

Postgame—Sacred Strategy

- When we can't see the end zone, run the play God calls.
- When we can't outrun our pain, let it fuel our purpose.
- When we can't forget our losses, let them inspire our giving.

Chain-Moving Challenge

This week, pick a specific area of life where you see yourself sometimes on the sidelines. What practical steps can you take to prepare you to get into the game?

Postgame Prayer

Eternal Victor,
Thank You for every story of redemption,
Every moment grace outscores judgment, and
Every life transformed by Your love.

Help us leave this discussion ready to play
In Your game of eternal consequence,
Scoring touchdowns that celebrate Your glory,
And advancing the ball toward heaven's goal line.

Through Christ, our Ultimate Champion,
Amen.

Personal Training Session

- What if these people decided to stay on the sidelines rather than get in the game?

- Moses, who spoke to God face to face, led the people of Israel out of Egypt, and received the Ten Commandments on the mountaintop

- Joshua, who led the people into the Promised Land and drove out the Canaanites

- Jesus, the Son of God, who took on humanity and lived and died and rose to take us to God

- Abraham, the father of Isaac and of many nations, who left Haran and went where God told him

- Noah, who headed the one small family to be saved from the great flood

- Esther, who risked her life to save the Jewish people from being killed

- Ruth, who left her pagan home and swore allegiance to her mother-in-law and to her God.

- Rahab, who hid the Israelite spies from the enemy and was saved when Jericho fell

Chain-Moving Challenge

Pick a specific area of life where you see yourself sometimes on the sidelines.

SWEET

- What practical steps can you take to prepare you to get into the game? _____

_____

- Notes: _____

_____

Game XII

Playing Injured

GRACE UNDER PRESSURE

For the training of the body has
a limited benefit, but godliness is
beneficial in every way.

1 TIMOTHY 4:8 (HCSB)

Pregame

Warmup Prayer

Divine Strengthener,
As we examine the paths of enhancement versus endurance,
Help us see beyond quick fixes to eternal victory.

SWEET

Like Eric Liddell, may we choose conviction over convenience, and
Like Christ, may we embrace the cross over shortcuts.

Guide our discussion to reveal Your sufficient grace,
That perfects itself in our weakness.

Through Christ, our Ultimate Champion,
Amen.

Chain-Moving Challenge Reflection

In response to the prompt: "Pick a specific area of life where you see yourself sometimes on the sidelines," what practical steps did you settle on to prepare you to get into the game?

Highlight Reel

In the quiet halls of Cooperstown, empty chairs tell a story of glory and fall, of records shattered and legacies tainted. The chapter opens with this poignant image of baseball's steroid era, using it as a gateway to explore humanity's eternal struggle with enhancement versus authenticity.

The narrative weaves three powerful storylines that illuminate different facets of this struggle. First, we visit Venice Beach's Gold's Gym, where Arnold Schwarzenegger and the bodybuilding culture openly embrace chemical enhancement, their honesty about steroids contrasting sharply with modern sports' denials. This transparency reveals something profound about human nature—our perpetual quest for shortcuts to glory.

The story then shifts to Winston Churchill in the war rooms beneath London, whiskey in hand, exemplifying how even history's giants wrestle with their dependencies. Churchill's famous quip about getting more from alcohol than it got from him becomes a window into human rationalization and self-deception.

At the heart of the chapter lies Dietrich Bonhoeffer's profound distinction between "cheap grace" and "costly grace." Like performance-enhancing drugs promising strength without struggle, cheap grace offers salvation without sacrifice, transformation without travail. The parallel between spiritual and physical enhancement becomes clear: both promise paradise without process, glory without grief.

The narrative finds its hero in Eric Liddell, the "Flying Parson," whose story transcends the familiar "Chariots of Fire" Olympic moment. His refusal to race on Sunday at the 1924 Olympics opens into a larger tale of authentic victory, culminating in his sacrificial service and death in a Japanese prison camp. Liddell's legacy offers a counterpoint to modern enhancement culture, showing how true victory often looks different from what the world celebrates.

The chapter concludes by returning to its opening metaphor, suggesting that heaven's record books will show different measures than Cooperstown's—not our shortcuts but our scars, not our enhancements but our endurance, not our supplements but our surrender. Like Christ choosing the cross over calling twelve legions of angels, true champions choose the harder right over the easier wrong, embracing weakness as the very vessel of divine strength.

This meditation on authenticity vs. enhancement ultimately reveals that the path to beauty was never meant to bypass the ugliness of the cross. In our age of instant solutions and chemical shortcuts, it reminds us that true transfiguration—whether in sports, faith, or life itself—comes not through avoiding struggle but through embracing it with grace.

GAMEDAY STRATEGY

True champions choose the harder right over the easier wrong, embracing weakness as the very vessel of divine strength.

Half-Time Huddle— Throw a SPIRAL

 S: Spirit-led Steadfastness

- How do we maintain authenticity in a culture that values quick results?
- What can we learn from Eric Liddell about choosing conviction over convenience?
- How do we resist the temptation of spiritual "performance enhancement?"

 P: Prayer

- How might our prayer life change if we truly embraced weakness as strength?
- What role does surrender play in authentic spiritual growth?
- What is intercessory prayer?

 I: Imagination

- How can we re-imagine weakness as a vessel for God's strength?
- What might our faith look like without "spiritual steroids?"
- How can we better envision victory through vulnerability?

R: Redemptive Relationships

- How do we support others choosing the harder right over the easier wrong?

- What can we learn from Bonhoeffer about costly versus cheap grace?

- How might we build communities that value authentic growth over quick fixes?

 A: Authentic Action

- What "spiritual shortcuts" do we need to surrender?

- How can we embrace the "sacred slowness" of genuine growth?

- What daily choices build authentic character rather than artificial strength?

 L: Life Story for a Living Legacy

- What kind of legacy are we creating through our choices about enhancement versus endurance?

- How can our struggles become testimonies of God's sufficient grace?

- What story will our lives tell about choosing the cross over shortcuts?

🌟 Every spiritual shortcut promises paradise but delivers prison. True transfiguration always involves:

- Death before resurrection
- Cross before crown
- Surrender before strength

Postgame—Wisdom

The Dependency Test

- Like Churchill's bottle, what dependencies do you rationalize?
- Where have you confused management with mastery?
- What idols promise power you can control?
- When has "I can handle it" become self-deception?

The Performance Review

- How does your spiritual "workout routine" reflect authenticity or enhancement?
- Where might you be trading tomorrow's legacy for today's glory?
- What asterisks would mark your spiritual achievements?

- How often do you choose the cross over the chemical?

The Desert Decision

- Which of Satan's three temptations resonates most with you?
- Where do you need to embrace the plateau instead of seeking the peak?
- How might God be using your current struggle to build authentic strength?

Coach's Corner—Mirror Check

- Where in your life are you seeking shortcuts to transfiguration?
- When have you chosen enhancement over engagement?
- What "spiritual steroids" tempt you most?
- How might your rush for results be hindering real growth?

Chain-Moving Challenge

This week, consider the statement: "Grace works through weakness, not workarounds."

Think of a time you depended on a workaround (with an I-can-fix-this attitude) rather than relying on God's grace? What do you think might have happened if you'd relied on God's grace in that situation? Do you think the outcome would have been different?

Postgame Prayer

Eternal Victor,

Thank You for the gift of weakness that becomes
  the vessel of Your strength.

Help us embrace our struggles as opportunities
  for Your grace and choose authentic growth
  over artificial enhancement.

May our lives tell stories of transformation through
  surrender rather than shortcuts.

Through Christ, who chose the cross,
Amen.

> Therefore I will boast all the more
> gladly of my weaknesses, so that
> the power of Christ may rest
> upon me.
>
> 2 CORINTHIANS 12:9 (ESV)

SWEET

Personal Training Session

Formation Check

Assess Your Enhancement Tendencies:

- Where do you rush results?
- When do you seek shortcuts?
- How do you rationalize spiritual steroids?

Identify Your Growth Zones:

- When do you have patience plateaus?
- Where are your surrender spots?
- What are your cross-carrying capabilities?

Final Play

When tempted by enhancement:

- Christ chose the cross over convenience.
- Real strength comes through surrender, not supplements.
- Christ didn't take a shortcut to save the world. Neither should we.

Chain-Moving Challenge

Consider the statement: Grace works through weakness, not workarounds.

- Can you think of a time you depended on a workaround (with an I-can-fix-this attitude) rather than relying on God's grace? _____

- What do you think might have happened if you'd relied on God's grace in that situation? _____

- Do you think the outcome would have been different? _____

- Notes: _____

Game XIII

The Ultimate Championship

BUILDING GOD'S TEAM

Pregame

Warmup Prayer

Divine Coach,
As we prepare to explore Your ultimate playbook,
Open our eyes to see beyond earthly
   championships to eternal victories waiting to
   be won.

Like Lamar Hunt, seeing possibility in a simple toy,
Help us recognize divine opportunities in daily
   moments.

Make us players, not spectators,

SWEET

In Your kingdom's greatest game.

Through Christ, our Ultimate Victor,
Amen.

Chain-Moving Challenge Reflection

Considering the fact that grace works through weakness, not workarounds:

- What times did you think of when you depended on a workaround [with an I-can-fix-this attitude] rather than relying on God's grace?
- What would have happened if you'd relied on God's grace in that situation? Would the outcome have been different?

Highlight Reel

The chapter opens with an origin story of the Super Bowl's name—born not in a corporate boardroom but in Lamar Hunt's living room, inspired by his daughter's Super Ball toy. This humble beginning blossoms into an exploration of how the Super Bowl has become USAmerica's most sacred sporting ritual, complete with its own liturgy, symbols, and communion.

The narrative then pivots to examine how this cultural phenomenon mirrors deeper spiritual truths. The Super Bowl becomes a lens through which to view our collective hunger for transcendence, from the cathedral-like stadiums to the jersey-vestments, from the processional Lombardi Trophy to the communion-like pregame feasts.

However, the chapter's real energy emerges in its second half, shifting from cultural analysis to kingdom application. Through a series of compelling real-life stories—from Sarah the barista to Linda the praying widow—we see how everyday disciples (or "gospellers") can "score touchdowns for eternity." Each narrative illustrates how ordinary moments can become rare opportunities for kingdom impact.

The chapter concludes by challenging readers to move beyond spectating to participation in God's ultimate championship team. It reframes daily opportunities—from difficult coworkers to social media platforms—as potential "end zones" for eternal impact, reminding us that while Super Bowl victories fade, kingdom touchdowns last forever.

GAMEDAY STRATEGY

The goal isn't just to win on Sunday. It's to live victoriously every day of the week.

Half-Time Huddle—Throw a SPIRAL

 S: Spirit-led Steadfastness

- What can we learn from the everyday "touchdown makers" described in the chapter?

- How do we stay alert to divine opportunities in ordinary moments?

- What's on your spiritual highlight reel this season?

 P: Prayer

- How might viewing prayer as a "play call from heaven" change our approach to intercession?

- What can we learn from Linda's phone ministry about faithful prayer?

- How can we better prepare ourselves spiritually for kingdom opportunities?

 I: Imagination

- How can we re-imagine our daily interactions as potential eternal end zones?

- What might our churches look like if we celebrated spiritual victories like Super Bowl moments?

- Where have you been playing it too safe in your faith?

 R: Redemptive Relationships

- How can we move from spectating to participating in others' spiritual journeys?
- What can we learn from Sarah, the barista, about divine interruptions?
- How might we better support each other in scoring "eternal touchdowns?"

 A: Authentic Action

- What "plays" is God calling us to make in our daily lives?
- How can we move from huddle to action in sharing our faith?
- What practical steps can we take to score touchdowns for eternity?

 L: Life Story for a Living Legacy

- What kind of eternal impact are we creating through our daily choices?
- How can our current struggles become tomorrow's ministry opportunities?
- What stories will future generations tell about our kingdom plays?

SWEET

Postgame—Team Workout

Preparation & Presence

- How do we prepare for worship with the same intensity that teams prepare for the Super Bowl?

- What would change if we studied our Bibles with the dedication of players studying their playbooks?

- Question for reflection: Do we bring more passion to the stadium or the sanctuary?

Community & Communion

- What can churches learn from how Super Bowl parties create instant community?

- How might we transform "fair weather fans" into faithful disciples?

- Discussion starter: What makes people paint their faces for football but shy away from public displays of faith?

Ritual & Remembrance

- Compare your church's communion service to the Super Bowl's pregame ceremonies. What parallels do you see?

- How do sports "testimonies" differ from spiri-

THE ULTIMATE CHAMPIONSHIP

tual testimonies?

- Group exploration: What rituals in your church could use a "halftime show" level of enthusiasm?

Victory & Defeat

- How does your faith community handle failure compared to how the NFL handles losing?
- What's the difference between "losing" in faith versus losing in football?
- Deep dive: Is there such a thing as a "spiritual underdog story?"

Chain-Moving Challenge

This week, intentionally:

- Practice spiritual alertness this week by intentionally looking for divine opportunities.
- Keep an "eternal scoreboard" of lives touched rather than personal achievements.
- Share your own story of failure and redemption with someone who needs hope.
- Turn interruptions into interventions by being open to divine audibles.
- Use your current resources and position for kingdom impact.

SWEET

Postgame Prayer

Lord of every field of play,
Help us run with purpose the race set before us.

When we fumble, remind us of your grace.

When we score, let our celebration honor you.

Keep us focused on the eternal game clock,
And help us play for an audience of One.

In Jesus' name,
Amen.

Personal Training— Training Camp Tips

- Study the Greatest Playbook Ever Written (Bible) daily.
- Practice spiritual conditioning (prayer & meditation).
- Run drills in forgiveness and grace.
- Work on your spiritual footwork (walking in faith).
- Strengthen your prayer receiver skills.
- Perfect your praise formations.

Coach's Corner

First Quarter: Personal Practice

- Start your day with a "pregame prayer."
- Create a "spiritual roster" of people supporting your faith journey.
- Develop your own "victory dance" of praise.

Second Quarter: Team Building

- Form a "spiritual special teams unit" (small group).
- Practice "holy huddles" (prayer circles).
- Run interference for others facing life's blitzes.

Third Quarter: Play Calling

- Audible into opportunities for witness.
- Watch for openings to share your faith story.
- Don't be afraid to call a "spiritual timeout."

Fourth Quarter: Championship Living

- Live like every day is the Super Bowl of faith.
- Remember you're playing for an eternal trophy.
- Keep your eyes on the ultimate end zone.

SWEET

Chain-Moving Challenge

This week, how did you intentionally:

- Practice spiritual alertness by intentionally looking for divine opportunities? _____

- Keep an "eternal scoreboard" of lives touched rather than personal achievements? _____

- Share your own story of failure and redemption with someone who needs hope? _____

- Turn interruptions into interventions by being open to divine audibles? _____

- Use your current resources and position for kingdom impact? _____

- Notes: _____

Bonus Formation

When life's defense lines up against you, remember the I.C.E. formations:

- In Christ Everything
- Intentional Christ Embodiment
- Infinite Celestial End zone
- The Super Bowl may last one day, but God's dynasty is eternal. Keep your head up, your heart open, and your faith strong. You're playing for the greatest Coach of all time. The whistle has blown. The game is on. Time to take the field for Christ.

PERSONAL TRAINING PRAYER

Eternal Champion,
Thank You for inviting us onto Your team,
For showing us that every day brings new opportunities to score touchdowns for Your kingdom.

Give us the courage to leave our comfortable huddles,
Wisdom to recognize heaven's audibles, and
Love to reach those in our fields of influence.

May we play not for temporal trophies,
But for eternal impact in Your name.

Through Christ, who secured the ultimate victory,
Amen.

Game XIV

When Tailgates Become Talegate Testaments

FELLOWSHIP IN THE PARKING LOT

Pregame

Warmup Prayer

Sacred Fire-Starter,

As we gather to discuss Your ways of bringing people together,

Help us see beyond the smoke of our grills to the holy ground You create in our gatherings.

Like You spoke through fire at Sinai and Pentecost,

SWEET

Speak to us through our everyday encounters.

May we recognize Your presence in every shared meal and story.

Through Christ, who makes all ground holy, Amen.

Chain-Moving Challenge Reflection

This past week, we looked for specific opportunities to make kingdom impacts. Do you have insights or victories to share?

- Practice spiritual alertness this week by intentionally looking for divine opportunities?
- Keep an "eternal scoreboard" of lives touched rather than personal achievements?
- Share your own story of failure and redemption with someone who needs hope?
- Turn interruptions into interventions by being open to divine audibles?
- Use your current resources and position for kingdom impact?

Highlight Reel

Game Fourteen weaves the ancient practice of gathering around a fire with modern tailgating culture, revealing a profound connection between sacred smoke and storytelling. Beginning with the observation that "stories flow where smoke rises," it traces this pattern from aboriginal dreamtime through biblical history to modern NFL parking lots.

The narrative explores how tailgating unknowingly taps into humanity's primal understanding of sacred space creation through fire and smoke. It draws parallels between ancient practices (Temple sacrifice, Pentecost) and modern gatherings, showing how the smoke from tailgate grills creates the same kind of "thin spaces" where stories naturally flow and community forms.

The chapter culminates in a detailed comparison of the two biblical Pentecosts (Sinai and Jerusalem), showing how God has consistently used fire and smoke to mark sacred encounters. It challenges readers to reclaim this understanding, suggesting that every grill could become an altar of gathering, every shared meal an opportunity for divine encounter.

Gameday Strategy

Good coaches, like good hosts, create environments where people can connect naturally.

Half-Time Huddle—Throw a SPIRAL

 S: Spirit-led Steadfastness

- What can we learn from the biblical pattern of God speaking through fire?

- How might viewing our gatherings as "holy ground" change how we approach them?

- What is your "talegate testimony"—a story best told over food and flame?

 P: Prayer

- How can we make our communal gatherings more intentionally spiritual?

- What role does shared food and fellowship play in our spiritual formation?

- How has the "smoke" of sacred spaces (incense, candles, cooking fires) shaped your own spiritual journey?

 I: Imagination

- How can we re-imagine our parking lots and backyards as sacred spaces?

- What might our church gatherings look like if we recovered this understanding of sacred smoke?

- How can we better create "thin spaces" where heaven and earth meet?

 R: Redemptive Relationships

- How do shared meals and stories create deeper community?
- What can we learn from tailgating culture about building authentic fellowship?
- When was the last time you experienced a profound moment of storytelling around a shared meal?

 A: Authentic Action

- How can we better use our homes and grills as gathering spaces for God's stories?
- What role should shared meals play in our ministry efforts?
- In what ways does your family preserve and pass down its most important stories? How can it do better?

 L: Life Story for a Living Legacy

- What stories are we creating around our own sacred fires?
- How can we better pass on faith through fellowship and food?

- How might your church re-imagine its gathering spaces to incorporate more elements of fire and feast?

POSTGAME

COACH'S CORNER—PREGAME RITUALS

Just as NFL teams create pregame rituals, church leaders can create meaningful "pre-worship" experiences:

- Train your team in the art of story-meals: hosting gatherings where food and narrative naturally mix.

- Look for ways to incorporate the sensory elements of smoke and fire into your worship spaces without losing their primal power.

- Good coaches, like good hosts, create environments where people can connect naturally.

SIDELINE WHISTLE

Don't rush to sanitize gathering spaces of their "smoke and fire" elements in the pursuit of relevance and the new.

- Have you had experiences where "smoke and fire" elements were changed or removed? What was the impact on the gathering space?

Avoid letting technology replace the power of face-to-face storytelling around shared flames.

- Do you currently have opportunities to have face-to-face storytelling? Where?

Be careful not to over-program meal gatherings; leave room for natural story flow.

- Do you wish you had more opportunities?
- How much programming of meal gatherings is enough?
- Is there a technique to planning a successful gathering that allows for a shift in plans to accommodate natural story flow and still make a meaningful experience?

Watch out for the tendency to separate sacred from the "profane" in your gathering practices. God made nothing "profane."

- Do you have different gathering "styles" depending on who you are with? If so, does having different styles for different gatherings impact your leadership effectiveness?

Smoke without a story, or a story without a sacred space, loses much of its power.

Chain-Moving Challenge

This week, as a coach, host, or player, participate in or create a time that has an environment where people can connect naturally.

Consider how we can recognize and create sacred spaces in everyday gatherings. What about implementing a "tailgate ministry" that creates sacred space in unexpected places?

Extra Point (Final Thought)

Just as God marked His most significant moments with fire and smoke—from Sinai to Pentecost—may we learn to mark our moments of ministry with the sacred smoke of hospitality and the holy fire of fellowship.

Postgame Prayer

Divine Host,
Thank You for every sacred space where smoke rises and stories flow,
Where hearts open and community forms.

Help us create more such spaces,
Where Your presence can be known through breaking bread and sharing life.

Make us aware of Your holy ground in parking lots and backyards alike.

Through Christ, our Ultimate Gathering Place, Amen.

Personal Training Plan

This week, spend time contemplating how to make space for personal stories. What stories from your life can you share? Begin making opportunities for "smoke and fire" in your gatherings, whether it is with your family, friends, church, or work.

Coach's Corner—Playbook on Prayer

Prayer is often compared to smoke or incense as a symbol of worship, intercession, and a pleasing aroma ascending to God. Here are some key passages that highlight the biblical imagery of prayer as a fragrant offering rising to God, much like incense in worship settings:

- Psalm 141:2
- Revelation 5:8 (where incense is directly identified as representing the prayers of the saints).
- Revelation 8:3–4
- Exodus 30:7–8

Postgame Plan (Practical Next Steps)

- Host a "Sacred Smoke Sunday" where your small group meets around a grill or fire pit.
- Start a tradition of lighting candles during family meals and sharing stories.
- Interview older members of your community about their memories of gathering around the fire and food.
- Create a "storytelling feast" calendar for your church or family.
- Experiment with incorporating more sensory elements in your worship spaces.

Two-Minute Drill (Quick Implementation Ideas)

- Place candles on your dinner table tonight.
- Call three friends and invite them to a backyard cookout.
- Start collecting family stories during meal times.
- Take photos of your next gathering around the fire or food.
- Write down one story you want future generations to remember.

FILM STUDY (RECOMMENDED RESOURCES)

From Tablet to Table by Leonard Sweet

Transcendence at the Table by Julia Hurlow

A Meal with Jesus by Tim Chester

The Gospel Comes with a House Key by Rosaria Butterfield

The Supper of the Lamb by Robert Farrar Capon

Making Room: Recovering Hospitality as a Christian Tradition by Christine D. Pohl

CHAIN-MOVING CHALLENGE

This week, we will participate in a time or event where people can connect naturally.

- How might we better create spaces where God's stories can naturally flow? _____

_____

- What practical steps can we take to make our gatherings more intentionally sacred?

_____

- Notes: _____

_____

SWEET

TRAINING SESSION PRAYER

Lord of the Burning Bush and Pentecost Fire,
Teach us to create spaces where Your stories can be shared.

Help us to recognize the sacred in the smoke of fellowship,
The holy in the gathering of Your people around flame and food.

Guide us in passing on Your story to the next generation,
Not just in words, but in the breaking of bread and the lighting of fires.

May our tables become altars and our grills become gathering places where Your Spirit moves as freely as smoke on the evening air.
Amen.

Game XV

More Than Games

FROM ARENA TO ALTAR

Pregame

Warmup Prayer

Eternal Storyteller,
As we explore the arenas of ancient and modern times,
Help us see beyond spectacle to significance,
Beyond entertainment to eternal truth,
Beyond the scoring to the Spirit,
Beyond the victory to the Vine.

Make us readers of Your signs,
Players in Your story in our gatherings and our games, and
Receivers of your grace.

SWEET

Finding true community where others see only crowds.

Through Christ, who turns spectators into family, Amen.

CHAIN-MOVING CHALLENGE REFLECTION

Last week, we participated in a time or event where people can connect naturally.

- Did you have an opportunity?
- Were you a coach, host, or player?
- How did your role affect how you were able to connect?
- Do you feel it is necessary to participate in different roles, or can you always be in the same role?

HIGHLIGHT REEL

Game Fifteen opens with a startling historical revelation about Gaius Appuleius Diocles, a Roman charioteer whose earnings would equate to roughly $15 billion today—dwarfing modern athletes' fortunes. This entry point launches a deep exploration of how sports transcend mere entertainment to become powerful shapers of society, both in ancient Rome and modern USAmerica.

Through examining the Roman-arena system, the

chapter reveals how sports became a complex intersection of politics, religion, and social control. The Romans understood something profound: control the games, and you control the narrative. From the Spartacan rebellion to the Nika Riots, the chapter shows how sports could both maintain and threaten empire.

The narrative then bridges to modern sports culture, particularly the NFL, demonstrating how our contemporary stadiums echo Rome's coliseums. Modern players become gladiators in cleats, while owners observe from luxury boxes like ancient patricians. The language of football itself—blitz, sudden death, bomb—reveals our continued fascination with stylized combat.

A central section examines Malcolm Butler's Super Bowl XLIX interception as a modern parable about pride, wisdom, and consequences. Through this lens, the chapter explores how single moments in sports can become teaching texts about larger spiritual and moral truths. Pete Carroll's inability to admit error becomes a lesson about pride's corrosive effects on community, while Butler's later benching in another Super Bowl illustrates the temporary nature of earthly glory.

The chapter culminates by contrasting Rome's "bread and circuses" with Jesus' approach to gathering and feeding people. Where Rome sought to distract and sedate, Jesus built genuine community. This comparison frames the modern tailgating culture as potentially offering something deeper than mere entertainment—authentic belonging and communion. Through shared meals, stories, and traditions, these parking lot gatherings can become sacred spaces where genuine community forms.

The final movement suggests that while we haven't abandoned our hunger for spectacle, we have the opportunity to transform it into something more meaningful. When strangers become family over shared food, when stories bind generations together, and when games become excuses for genuine connection, these moments echo Jesus' way of making family out of foreigners.

The chapter ultimately challenges readers to recognize and create these opportunities for genuine community, suggesting that our modern sports culture, while often mimicking Rome's entertainment complex, also offers unique opportunities for authentic connection and meaning-making that transcends mere spectacle.

Through this historical and theological lens, the chapter argues that sports remain powerful shapers of social narrative and community, but their ultimate value lies not in the spectacle they create but in the connections they enable and the stories they help us tell about ourselves and our place in the larger human story.

Gameday Strategy

The real victory isn't on the scoreboard but in the story we're telling with our lives.

Half-Time Huddle— Throw a SPIRAL

 S: Spirit-led Steadfastness

- How do we maintain spiritual authenticity in a culture of spectacle?
- What can we learn from Rome's mistakes and the NFL's community-building success?
- When has a sports moment taught you about grace?

 P: Prayer

- How might viewing our gatherings as sacred spaces change our approach to community?
- What can we learn from Jesus's approach to feeding and gathering people?

- How can we pray for our sports culture to become more life-giving?

 I: Imagination

- How can we re-imagine our stadiums and gatherings as opportunities for genuine community?

- What might our churches learn from the community-building aspects of sports culture?

- How can we make our churches as welcoming as a tailgate party?

 R: Redemptive Relationships

- What can we learn from tailgating culture about genuine fellowship?

- How might we better use shared experiences to build lasting connections?

- What's the difference between a fan base and a faith community?

 A: Authentic Action

- What practical steps can we take to move from spectacle to substance in our gatherings?

- How can we create more opportunities for genuine community building?

- What role should shared meals and stories play in our ministry?

 L: Life Story for a Living Legacy

- What kind of stories are we creating in our communities?
- How can we better pass on faith through shared experiences?
- What legacy of gathering and belonging are we building?

Postgame

⚠ *Warning Flags*

Have you witnessed situations where these warnings were warranted?

- Don't substitute programs for praise.
- Avoid mistaking quietness for reverence.
- Watch out for the dignity disease and respectability routine that kills holy joy.
- Beware of celebrating structure over Spirit.
- Don't let fear of excess kill genuine expression.

SWEET

⏲ Two-Minute Warning— Special Teams

- Sports can be sacred if we see them rightly.
  Community matters more than competition.
- Grace covers both victory and defeat.
- Jesus offers more than bread and circuses.
- Every game tells God's story.

🎙 Chain-Moving Challenge

The real victory isn't on the scoreboard but in the story we're telling with our lives. This week, when we gather around our arenas, let's remember we're really gathering around something much older—the human need for story, community, redemption, and grace.

Postgame Prayer

Divine Host,
Thank You for every space where strangers
    become family, and
Games become gateways to grace.

Help us create communities that offer more than
    bread and circuses,
That point to Your eternal feast.

May our gatherings echo with Your presence and our stories resound with Your truth.

Through Christ, our Ultimate Victor,
Amen.

Personal Training— Game Film Review

First Quarter: Ancient Echoes

- How do today's sports "temples" compare to ancient Rome's?
- What are we really worshiping when we worship sports?
- Where do you see signs of "bread and circuses" in your own life?
- How can we distinguish between healthy enjoyment and unhealthy worship of sports?

Second Quarter: Contemporary Arena

- In what ways does your team loyalty reflect or replace religious devotion?
- How do you read God's signs in sports moments?
- What spiritual lessons have you learned from game-changing plays?
- Where do you see resurrection stories in sports?

Third Quarter: Pride and Fall

- When have you been Pete Carroll, unable to admit a mistake?
- When have you been Malcolm Butler, going from hero to forgotten?
- How does your community handle failure in leadership?
- What's the difference between grace and enabling in sports leadership?

Fourth Quarter: Beyond the Game

- How can your church create community as effectively as sports do?
- What would "real bread" look like in your congregation?
- How can we turn spectacle into sacrament?
- Where do you see Jesus in the sports stories of our time?

Coach's Corner—Implementation Strategy

This Week

- Notice where sports intersect with spirituality in your life.

- Practice seeing sacred stories in sports moments.
- Look for opportunities to transform spectatorship into fellowship.

This Month

- Start a sports ministry that focuses on community over competition.
- Create a "Tailgate Testimony" series in your small group.
- Develop ways to make church as welcoming as a stadium.

This Season

- Transform your game-watching gatherings into story-sharing communities.
- Build bridges between sports fans and faith seekers.
- Create new traditions that combine the best of both worlds.

Chain-Moving Challenge

The real victory isn't on the scoreboard but in the story we're telling with our lives. This week, when we gather around our arenas, let's remember we're really gathering around something much older—

SWEET

the human need for story, community, redemption, and grace.

- What story are you telling with your life? _____
  _____
- Notes: _____
  _____

Game XVI

Beyond the Goalposts

From Kickoff to Kingdom Come

Pregame

Warmup Prayer

Divine Celebration Starter,
As we prepare to explore Your call to holy enthusiasm,
Awaken in us the courage to celebrate eternal victories with the same passion we bring to temporal ones.

Like the father who ran to his prodigal son,
Help us shed our dignity for Your glory.

May we rediscover the joy that made angels leap

and saints shout their praise through the ages.

Through Christ, who turns every moment into celebration,
Amen.

Chain-Moving Challenge Reflection

The real victory isn't on the scoreboard but in the story we're telling with our lives. Last week, when we gathered around our arenas, we remembered we're really gathering around something much older—the human need for story, community, redemption, and grace.

What story are you telling with your life?

Highlight Reel

"Game Sixteen: Beyond the Goalposts" weaves three major themes: the irony of lost celebration in modern churches, the importance of reading and responding to divine moments, and the call to reclaim authentic spiritual enthusiasm. It opens with a pointed observation about how Methodist churches, once known for their "shouting" spirituality and mocked as "Enthusiasts," have become bastions of quiet restraint while members save their enthusiasm for sports stadiums and music concerts.

Through powerful contrasting narratives—J. J. Watt vs. Joel Osteen during Hurricane Harvey, three popes facing their historical moments, and the Bound Brook Six's bold faith declaration—the chapter illustrates how character reveals itself in crucial moments. The narrative builds toward a compelling call for Christians to reclaim their heritage of holy celebration, suggesting that enthusiasm in worship isn't just permitted but is essential for spiritual warfare and kingdom advancement.

The chapter concludes by challenging readers to choose between maintaining dignified restraint and embracing holy abandonment in their faith expression, arguing that true victory in Jesus demands the same passion we bring to sporting events—and more, because these celebrations count for eternity.

Gameday Strategy

Every moment of spiritual victory deserves at least as much celebration as a touchdown. Heaven is shouting. So should we.

Half-Time Huddle— Throw a SPIRAL

 S: Spirit-led Steadfastness

- How do we maintain authentic enthusiasm in our faith expression?

- What keeps us from celebrating spiritual victories as passionately as sports victories?
- How do you respond differently to touchdowns on earth versus touchdowns in eternity?

 P: Prayer

- How might viewing heaven as a celebrating community change our approach to prayer?
- How can we pray more boldly and enthusiastically?
- Where have comfort and dignity replaced holy enthusiasm?

 I: Imagination

- When do you feel most free to express joy in worship?
- What keeps you from celebrating spiritual victories more openly?
- How can we better envision and create moments of holy abandonment?

 R: Redemptive Relationships

- What can we learn from the early Methodists about combining passion and purpose?
- How might our celebration draw others to faith?

- What spiritual victory have you witnessed but failed to celebrate?

 A: Authentic Action

- What practical steps can we take to reclaim our heritage of holy enthusiasm?
- In crisis moments, are you more like J. J. Watt or Joel Osteen?
- How can we better respond to God's moments like J. J. Watt did?

 L: Life Story for a Living Legacy

- What kind of celebratory heritage are we creating?
- How can our authentic enthusiasm inspire the next generation?
- When was the last time you took a holy risk?

Postgame—
Implementation Ideas

Start a "Victory Journal" today.

- What types of things would you include in this journal?

Plan a "Heritage of Holy Noise" Sunday.

- What would this look like?

SWEET

- What part of your community could you implement this in?

Create a "Celebration Team" in your church.

- Does your church have a celebration team?
- Does celebration naturally happen in your church?
- What kinds of things would you love to see celebrated?

Practice one new expression of joy this week.

- What are some ways you currently express joy?
- Is there a new way of expressing joy you would like to implement?

Share a spiritual victory story at your next meal.

- Where do you share meals with other people?
- What is a spiritual victory story you could share?

Chain-Moving Challenge

This week, look for and celebrate one spiritual victory each day.

Postgame Prayer

Lord of the Dance,
Who set the stars spinning in their courses and
    taught David to leap before Your ark,

Restore to us the joy of holy celebration.

Free us from false dignity,
Release us from spiritless religion,
Teach us again to shout Your praise,
Until heaven's bleachers and earth's stadiums ring
    with one voice of triumph.

Make us again Your shouting people,
Your celebrating saints,
Your joyful disciples.

For the touchdowns yet to come and the victories
    yet to celebrate,
We pray with lifted voices,
Amen.

Personal Training— Coach's Corner

Special Teams: Celebration Coordinator

- Someone specifically tasked with marking and amplifying spiritual victories
- Track and announce salvation decisions.
- Create celebration rituals for baptisms.
- Organize spontaneous praise moments.
- Train others in holy hilarity.

Postgame Plan (Practical Next Steps)

First Quarter: Personal Revival

- Research your denomination's historic expressions of joy.
- Practice celebration in private prayer.
- Journal spiritual victories daily.
- Share your faith story with holy enthusiasm.

Second Quarter: Family Focus

- Create family celebration rituals for spiritual milestones.
- Tell stories of God's faithfulness with excitement.
- Practice praise together without embarrassment.
- Make spiritual victories as exciting as sports wins.

Third Quarter: Church Culture

- Start a "Holy Noise" training program.
- Institute "Celebration Sundays" monthly.
- Create space for testimonies and praise.
- Teach the theology of celebration.

Fourth Quarter: Community Impact

- Take celebration outside church walls.
- Partner with other churches for praise events.

- Create public ceremonies for spiritual victories.
- Make community service a celebration.

Film Study (Recommended Resources)

The Holy Spirit and Revival by John Wesley

Celebration of Discipline by Richard Foster

The Celtic Way of Prayer by Esther de Waal

Postmodern and Wesleyan?: Responses by Leonard Sweet , editors Jay Richard Akkerman, Thomas J. Oord, and Brent D. Peterson

The Greatest Story Never Told: Revive Us Again by Leonard Sweet

The Autobiography of Peter Cartwright (early Methodist circuit rider)

Extra Points

- Share your faith story with holy enthusiasm.
- Research your tradition's "celebration roots."
- Practice one new expression of spiritual joy.
- Organize a celebration for someone's milestone in their life story.

SWEET

⏺ CHAIN-MOVING CHALLENGE

This week, look for and celebrate one spiritual victory each day.

_____

_____

_____

_____

Game XVII

LATERALS OF LOVE

PASSING FAITH THROUGH LIFE'S CHAOS

PREGAME

WARMUP PRAYER

Divine Playmaker,

As we prepare to explore Your kingdom in motion,

Help us see beyond apparent defeat to eternal possibility.

Like those California players who kept the ball alive,

May we learn to trust, to lateral, and to advance Your kingdom through unexpected channels.

Give us courage to stay in the play

Even when the opposing band takes the field.

SWEET

Through Christ, who turns endings into
  beginnings,
Amen.

CHAIN-MOVING CHALLENGE REFLECTION

What were some of the spiritual victories you celebrated last week?

HIGHLIGHT REEL

Game Seventeen, the final chapter, distills the book's central themes through the powerful lens of "The Play"—the legendary 1982 California-Stanford game that showcased the intersection of divine possibility and human persistence. This iconic moment, where five laterals and an encounter with a bewildered trombonist led to an impossible victory, serves as a rich metaphor for how God's kingdom moves the chains in our world.

The chapter begins by emphasizing the crucial distinction between "working" and "playing" football, suggesting that the highest forms of both athletic and spiritual beauty emerge not from laborious effort but from the joy of play. Through this framework, it explores how moments of apparent defeat often become platforms for God's most spectacular work.

The narrative carefully unpacks the spiritual significance of each element of "The Play": the five laterals representing moments of trust and the willing surrender of control, the Stanford defenders symbolizing life's obstacles, and even the trombonist becoming an unwitting participant in God's unfolding drama. Each component illustrates how the kingdom of God advances not through raw power but through surrender, trust, and the willingness to keep believing when all seems lost.

The chapter then broadens its scope to show how this pattern appears throughout scripture and contemporary life—from Moses at the Red Sea to modern-day ministry in hospital waiting rooms and food pantries. It demonstrates how God's kingdom moves forward through unexpected channels, often using our apparent obstacles as stepping stones to victory.

These themes culminate in a powerful reflection on how we're called to carry the gospel—not as something to be cradled safely, but as a message to be constantly passed on, transfiguring both the carrier and the message as the gospel carries us. The chapter emphasizes that just as each Cal player had to adjust their position and grip to keep the play alive, we too must be willing to reorient our lives to effectively pass on Christ's love.

The narrative concludes by bringing together the book's overarching message: that in God's kingdom, like in that memorable game, victory often comes through unexpected means, persistence trumps power, and what appears to be the end can become a divine beginning. Through practical examples—from businesswomen mentoring young professionals to recovering addicts sharing their testimonies—it shows how "The Play" continues in countless ways through faithful believers who refuse to give up even when the opposing band takes the field.

This final chapter serves not just as a conclusion but as a commissioning, challenging readers to take their place in God's ongoing "play," ready to receive and pass on the gospel with the understanding that in God's kingdom, the game is never truly over until God says so.

GAMEDAY STRATEGY

What appears to be the end can become a divine beginning, because in God's kingdom, the game is never truly over until God says so.

HALF-TIME HUDDLE— THROW A SPIRAL

 S: SPIRIT-LED STEADFASTNESS

- How do we maintain faith when the scoreboard says: "game over?"

- What can we learn from "The Play" about trusting God's process?
- How do we keep spiritual momentum alive in challenging times?

 P: PRAYER

- How might viewing faith as "play" rather than "work" change our prayer life?
- What role does trust play in passing on our faith to others?
- How can we pray with more expectancy for divine possibilities?

 I: IMAGINATION

- Like the California players who kept the ball alive through multiple laterals, where in your life might God be asking you to "keep the play alive" despite apparent defeat?
- What "impossible" situations are you facing that might require unexpected solutions?
- Who are the teammates in your life ready to receive your "lateral pass" when you're about to be tackled by life's challenges?

R: Redemptive Relationships

- How do we effectively "lateral" our faith to others?
- What can we learn from team play about kingdom advancement?
- How might our obstacles become part of others' testimonies?

 A: Authentic Action

- What practical steps can we take to keep God's play alive in our sphere?
- What does kingdom advancement look like in our context?
- What role should the church play in healing social divisions?

 L: Life Story for a Living Legacy

- When did you last approach your faith with the joy and freedom of "play" rather than the burden of "work?"
- How might viewing your spiritual life through the lens of "play" change your approach to church, prayer, and service?
- What barriers prevent you from experiencing the freedom of spiritual "play?"

Postgame

For the kingdom of God is not a matter of talk but of power.

1 CORINTHIANS 4:20 [NIV]

The Championship Drive

Choose one area this week where you will:

- Replace "work" with "play" in your spiritual life.
- Make an unexpected "lateral pass" to keep hope alive.
- Cross a divide to engage with someone different from you.
- Trust God's playbook even when the odds seem impossible.

Chain-Moving Challenge

This week, consider these questions: How can we re-imagine obstacles as opportunities in God's kingdom? What might our faith look like if we truly believed no situation was hopeless? What "echo chambers" have you created in your own life? When was the last time you genuinely engaged with someone whose viewpoints differ significantly from yours? How can you maintain your convictions while building bridges across ideological divides?

Postgame Prayer

Eternal Victor,
Thank You for every moment where You turn
    apparent endings into divine beginnings.

Help us remember that in Your kingdom,
The final whistle never sounds until You say so.

Make us faithful players in Your grand game,
Ready to receive and pass on Your grace,
Until that day when every knee bows and every
    tongue confesses Your victory.

Through Christ, our Ultimate Champion,
Amen.

Personal Training Session

Personal Formation (First Quarter)

- Set aside fifteen minutes each day this week to "play" with God through unstructured prayer or meditation.

- List three "lateral passes" you could make to keep moving forward in areas where you feel stuck.

- Identify one source of news or information from

a perspective different from your usual choices.

Family Focus (Second Quarter)

- Plan a family activity that emphasizes play and cooperation over competition.
- Share stories of times when your family had to work together to overcome obstacles.
- Create a "lateral list" of family members' strengths and how you can support each other.

Professional Purpose (Third Quarter)

- Look for opportunities to bridge divisions in your workplace.
- Practice seeing colleagues with opposing viewpoints as teammates rather than opponents.
- Identify ways to bring playfulness and joy into your professional responsibilities.

Kingdom Impact (Fourth Quarter)

- Find one concrete way to engage with someone from "the other side" of a political or social divide.
- Start a prayer journal focusing on unity and reconciliation in your community.
- Look for unexpected ways God might be working in situations that seem hopeless.

SWEET

OVERTIME OPPORTUNITIES

Study Scriptures:

- Philippians 2:1–4 (Unity in Christ)
- Romans 12:16–18 (Living in harmony)
- 1 Corinthians 12:12–27 (One body, many parts)
- Matthew 5:43–48 (Loving enemies)

CHAIN-MOVING CHALLENGE

This week, consider these questions:

- How can we re-imagine obstacles as opportunities in God's kingdom? _____

_____

- What might our faith look like if we truly believed no situation was hopeless? _____

_____

- What "echo chambers" have you created in your own life? _____

_____

- When was the last time you genuinely engaged with someone whose viewpoints differ significantly from yours? _____

_____

- How can you maintain your convictions while building bridges across ideological divides? ____
- Notes: _____

Victory *Celebration*

THE CHAMPIONSHIP MINDSET

I have fought the good fight, I have finished the race, I have kept the faith. Now there is in store for me the crown of righteousness, which the Lord, the righteous Judge, will award to me on that day—and not only to me, but also to all who have longed for his appearing.

2 TIMOTHY 4:7-8 (NIV)

As we reach the final moments of our exploration of faith and football, we gather for one last sacred huddle. Throughout history, great coaches have given legendary locker room speeches, and devoted believers have crafted timeless prayers. This prayer brings these traditions together, speaking both the language of the gridiron and the eternal truths of grace.

Like a well-designed play that brings together every element of the game, this prayer weaves the metaphors of football with the deepest longings of our hearts, reminding us that on God's field, we're all playing for something far greater than any earthly championship.

THE GRIDIRON PRAYER:

Almighty God, Creator, Redeemer, and Great Life Coach,
You who designed the perfect playbook in Your Word, and
Sent Your Son as the ultimate quarterback of our salvation,
We come before Your throne of grace with hearts full of gratitude.

Lord of every field and every contest,
You who turn our fumbles into opportunities,
Our defeats into wisdom, and
Our victories into humble praise—
We thank You for the game of life You've given us to play.

Just as Jesus broke through the defensive line of death and scored the winning touchdown of

VICTORY CELEBRATION

resurrection,
Help us run our race with perseverance,
Following the chalk lines of Your commandments,
And keeping our eyes fixed on the goal posts of Your Kingdom.

When we are tackled by doubt,
Grant us the strength to lateral the ball of faith to our brothers and sisters.

When we face fourth and long in life's toughest moments,
Give us courage to trust Your game plan.

When we're tempted to retreat to our own end zone of comfort,
Push us forward into the open field of Your mission.

Unite us as one team under Your banner,
Breaking down the divisions of jersey colors and team loyalties,
Until we see that in Your stadium, we all play for Your glory.

Make us both good winners and gracious losers,
Knowing that every game is but practice for eternity.

Coach our hearts to love like special teams—
Sacrificing our position so others might advance.

SWEET

Train our minds like quarterbacks—
Reading the defense of deception and choosing truth.

Strengthen our spirits like offensive lines—
Standing firm against the blitz of temptation.

In the fourth quarter of our lives,
When the clock of mortality winds down,
Help us remember that through Christ's victory,
We play in a game that never truly ends,
Where every touchdown scored in love echoes in the hallways of heaven.

And when the final whistle blows on our earthly game,
May we cross the goal line of faith into Your eternal end zone of glory,
Where we'll join the greatest cloud of witnesses in the forever celebration of Your championship love.

We pray this in the name of Jesus Christ,
The MVP of all creation,
Who took the field of humanity,
Ran the play of perfect obedience,
And won the Super Bowl of salvation for all who put their trust in Him.

To You be the victory,
The trophy, and

VICTORY CELEBRATION

The glory,
Forever and ever.
Amen.[2]

---

[2]. This prayer was written with the "corporate anthem" of the dystopian sports and society drama *Rollerball* (1975) playing in the background as its anti-type. James Caan magnificently plays superstar "Jonathan E."

Scripture Versions

Scripture quotations marked NIV are taken from the Holy Bible, New International Version®, NIV®. Copyright © 1973, 1978, 1984, 2011 by Biblica, Inc.™ Used by permission of Zondervan. All rights reserved worldwide. www.zondervan.com. The "NIV" and "New International Version" are trademarks registered in the United States Patent and Trademark Office by Biblica, Inc.™

Scripture quotations marked KJV are taken from the Holy Bible, King James Version.

Scripture quotations marked ASV are taken from the Holy Bible, American Standard Version.

Scripture quotations marked NKJV are from the New King James Version.® Copyright © 1982 by Thomas Nelson, Inc. Used by permission. All rights reserved.

Scripture quotations marked ESV are from The Holy Bible, English Standard Version® ESV®, copyright © 2001 by Crossway, a publishing ministry of Good News Publishers. Used by permission. All rights reserved.

Scripture quotations marked HCSB are taken from the Holman Christian Standard Bible®, Copyright © 1999, 2000, 2002, 2003 by Holman Bible Publishers. Used by permission. Holman Christian Standard Bible®, Holman CSB®, and HCSB® are federally registered trademarks of Holman Bible Publishers.

Additional Study Questions

These questions are optional and provide opportunity for further reflection.

- How might we better support others in their practice of faith and character formation?
- What would your life look like if you lived it on "Lombardi Time?"
- How can we maintain kingdom focus in a culture obsessed with temporal victories?
- How can we better envision kingdom impact in our spheres of influence?
- Who's in your faith fantasy league (support system)?
- What spiritual equipment needs upgrading in your life?
- What's your game plan for deeper growth in faith?
- How do you unite passion for sports with spiritual priorities?
- How do we balance appreciation for sports with a proper spiritual perspective?
- How can we better create spaces where strangers become family?

- How do we build an authentic community beyond mere entertainment?
- When was the last time you celebrated a spiritual victory with the same enthusiasm as a sports win?
- How can we better read and respond to God's moments?
- What role does spiritual celebration play in warfare against darkness?
- What role does spiritual celebration play in warfare against darkness?
- How can we re-imagine our churches as centers of authentic celebration?
- What might our worship look like if we brought stadium-level enthusiasm to spiritual victories?
- How do we build communities that celebrate spiritual victories authentically?
- What might it look like to celebrate spiritual victories in our daily lives?
- How has your church's expression of joy changed over generations?
- What stories of bold faith will others tell about us?
- How can we maintain strong convictions while building bridges with those who disagree?

ADDITIONAL STUDY QUESTIONS

- How can we better pass on faith in our daily interactions?
- How can we keep our focus on eternal victories rather than temporal wins?
- What if we saw all of life as a prayer, and started living and being "The Lord's Prayer?"
- What does it mean to give our strengths and gifts "to the fullest," or as Oswald Chambers put it, from notes taken by his wife Biddy Chambers, "my utmost for his highest?"
- This week, pick a specific plateau or struggle you're facing. How can you pray through it rather than seek a shortcut?

CONNECT WITH LEONARD

For more from Leonard Sweet:

Websites:
- www.leonardsweet.com
- www.preachthestory.com
- www.sanctuaryseaside.com

Instagram: @leonard.sweet

Facebook:
- facebook.com/lensweet
- facebook.com/preachthestory
- facebook.com/sanctuaryseaside

Twitter: @lensweet

YouTube: www.youtube.com/@leonardsweet1

Podcast: www.leonardsweet.com/podcasts

Napkin Scribbles Podcast:

Spotify:
- https://open.spotify.com/show/2vt6wEi70dQEpW37CypfvY

iTunes:
- https://podcasts.apple.com/gb/podcast/napkin-scribbles-a-podcast-by-leonard-sweet/id1436743015

www.ingramcontent.com/pod-product-compliance
Lightning Source LLC
Chambersburg PA
CBHW072152070526
44585CB00015B/1101